TREATING THE TROUBLESOME

The ethical problems
of compulsory medical treatment
for socially unacceptable behaviour

Report of a Working Party

CSS
REPORT

ISBN Hb 0 906503 08 6
Pb 0 906503 07 8
Set in 9pt Century
Printed by
Calverts North Star Press,
55 Mount Pleasant, London WC1X 0AE

About the Council

The Council for Science and Society, a registered charity, was formed in 1973 with the object of "promoting the study of, and research into, the social effects of science and technology, and of disseminating the results thereof to the public".

The Council's primary task is to stimulate informed public discussion in the field of "the social responsibility of the scientist". It seeks to identify developments in science and technology whose social consequences lie just over the horizon, where no full-scale debate has yet begun, but where intensive analysis of the present (and probable future) "state of the art", and of the foreseeable social consequences, can suggest a range of possible responses to those who will sooner or later have to take the necessary decisions. The Council carries out this task in a number of different ways, including the organisation of conferences, seminars and colloquia.

Major studies are conducted by ad hoc working parties, composed — like the Council itself — of experts in the respective fields, together with lawyers, philosophers and others who can bring a wide range of skills and experience to bear on their subject. The results of these studies are published in the form of reports such as this one. It is the Council's hope that these will help others to work out the most appropriate solutions to these problems in the course of a responsible public debate, conducted at leisure on the best information available, rather than by the hurried, ill-informed and ill-considered process which is apt to occur if the community does not become aware of a problem until it is too late.

The Council is greatly indebted to the Trustees of the Leverhulme Trust Fund for their continued support.

The Council welcomes all suggestions of further subjects for study.

COUNCIL FOR SCIENCE AND SOCIETY,
3/4 St Andrews Hill,
London EC4V 5BY
Tel: 01-236-6723

Membership of the Working Party

David Sullivan Q.C.	(Convenor)
Mary Appleby C.B.E., J.P.	Director, National Association for Mental Health (MIND), 1951-74.
The Hon. Mrs.S.M.Baring J.P.	Member of the Parole Board for England and Wales.
Professor Archie Duncan D.S.C.	Professor (Emeritus) of Medical Education, University of Edinburgh.
Professor John Gunn	Professor of Forensic Psychiatry, Institute of Psychiatry.
Professor Malcolm Lader	Professor of Clinical Pharmacology, Institute of Psychiatry.
David Lloyd Thomas	Dept. of Philosophy, Bedford College, University of London.
Paul Sieghart	(Council Representative) Chairman of the Executive Committee, *Justice*.
Kenneth Denbigh	Director, Council for Science and Society.
John Hillier	(Secretary) Secretary, Council for Science and Society.

Contents

Preface

Many of our ills are self-inflicted, and could be cured by elementary common sense and good will. But there are some unhappy elements of the human condition that appear irreducible. There have always been some people who seem incapable of adapting their behaviour to normal civil society. From culture to culture, from epoch to epoch, the way they are treated ranges from exasperated tolerance to self-righteous cruelty: but none of these treatments has yet made much difference to the incidence of the phenomenon, or its disruptive effects.

Will this distressing social problem always be with us? Might we not one day discover an effective means of putting such people right? Think how much misery this would save, both to the individuals concerned and to all who have dealings with them.

The question might seem to be one about the technical capabilities of medical science. But real human problems can seldom be "fixed" without reference to non-technical principles and values. We must always look underneath the superficial question of whether we actually have any technique that will cure the immediate ill, and ask what the repercussions of such a treatment might be, and how they might be controlled. This particular issue goes far beyond the delicate medical ethics of getting the "informed consent", of an emotionally, mentally, or socially disturbed patient, to a dangerous treatment whose outcome might well be beneficial but cannot be guaranteed. It draws us into the deepest waters of our conceptions of human personality, and amongst the oldest and thorniest dilemmas of politics, such as the extent to which an individual may be compelled to suffer in order that society might be saved trouble.

Until recently, the issue discussed in this Report was more or less academic. But ever since the foundation of the Council for Science and Society in 1973 we have been well aware that progress in medical science was bringing it closer to reality. As the Report makes clear, unacceptable social behaviour cannot yet be "fixed" reliably and safely, but neurosurgeons, pharmacologists, psychiatrists and other experts claim that they are fast developing effective techniques for intervening in the workings of the human mind or brain so as to modify individual behaviour in more or less predictable ways. Here, then, was an issue lying right in the middle of our sphere of interests, where science, ethics and law overlap and intertwine. Even if (by contrast with the United States) it had not yet become a matter for public debate in Britain, it could erupt at any time, and ought to be thought about very seriously well before then.

In fact, because it is such a complex and controversial topic, it took us much longer than we expected to get together a Working Party of people both competent and willing to argue it out in sufficient depth. Under the leadership of the convenor, David Sullivan Q.C., they have now produced this Report, to which they have all contributed and to which they all subscribe. Fortunately, it was completed just in time for the public debate that we knew must eventually take place, for legislation on these issues will probably be included in the new Mental Health Bill that the Government is said to be planning to present to Parliament very soon.

In commending this Report for publication, the Council does not, of course, unanimously endorse every step in the Working Party's argument, and every detail of its proposals. But although we do not pretend to have a consensus on the precise actions that society ought to take on this very controversial issue, we are satisfied that this is a fair account of the technical "state of the art", the principles of medicine, ethics, law, and public administration that bear upon it, and the foreseeable consequences of various courses of action that might be followed in dealing with it. And that is what we have tried to do — to help the formation of public policies by providing reliable facts and rational views for responsible and informed public debate and decision.

As ever, it is a pleasure to acknowledge the financial support of the Leverhulme Trust Fund, together with an anonymous gift from a major charitable foundation, which made this study possible.

JOHN ZIMAN

1

The Theme of this Report

Every society has limits of tolerance beyond which it regards some kinds of conduct as unacceptable. But the limits of tolerance of anti-social or deviant behaviour vary widely, both as between different societies, and within the same society at different times. For instance, in the United Kingdom attitudes to homosexual conduct between consenting adults have changed significantly of recent years: so have attitudes to the taking of drugs.

Societies vary too in ascribing moral responsibility to the kind of behaviour they regard as unacceptable; and even psychiatrists, who are specialists in the study of the mind, can still disagree profoundly about whether, in any given case, an individual is primarily "mad" or "bad".

Far too little is yet known about the causes of such behaviour: genetics, inadequate parents, broken homes, and prolonged unemployment are only some of the candidates that have their supporters. But whatever the causes might be, we have not yet found any effective prophylactic measures against them.

Small wonder then that opinion is sharply divided about whether, and how, such behaviour should be modified once it manifests itself — by treatment for the "mad", or reform or punishment for the "bad". Until quite recently, neither treatment, punishment, nor reform involved any high or complex level of technology. But that situation is changing fast as a variety of scientific techniques to modify human behaviour has started to make rapid progress. These have been developed within the disciplines of pharmacology, surgery, medicine and psychology. In this country at least, they are still only used to treat the sick — that is, those whose undesirable behaviour is thought to be associated with a demonstrable malfunctioning of some part of the organism. But whenever new technologies are developed, there is a temptation to use them for purposes for which they were not originally designed — as a "technical fix" for other problems which have hitherto proved intractable.

That temptation could prove to be particularly strong in the control of socially unacceptable behaviour. Many people in many societies would feel more secure if there were fewer deviants, whether their behaviour is classified as deliberately criminal, or due to mental illnesses for which they are not responsible. Society would be glad to be delivered from a whole range of murderers, psychopaths, muggers, child molesters and thieves, especially as the crime statistics continue to rise. Some would also welcome the disappearance of eccentrics with odd life styles, who do not conform to accepted norms of behaviour or political opinion. And deviants also present other problems, such as their containment in prisons and hospitals where discipline can all too easily be disrupted by a small number of violent trouble-makers.

That the temptation to use the new technologies to solve such problems is real has been amply demonstrated by the use to which some special Soviet psychiatric hospitals have been put. But disturbing accounts have come from other parts of the world too, including North America, where cases of "treatment" of prisoners for their own good — but perhaps more for the good of the society against which they have offended — have been reported.

Even British psychiatric hospitals have not been without their occasional scandals — sometimes, but not always, shown to have been founded on fact by a subsequent official investigation. The temptation to manipulate and control deviant behaviour, in the interests of the greater safety of the community, certainly exists. The question is whether it should be guarded against. That is one of the reasons why we have prepared this Report.

Another reason is the general unease which we have sensed in the public at large about how minds can be bent by mysterious new techniques, and a pervasive ignorance of what exactly such techniques involve.

It seems clear that there are strong public reactions against any interference with what we call the citadel of an individual's personality, whether such interference is committed in the name of medicine or of social control. Some of these reactions are rational, some are emotional. Most people believe that the citadel of the mind is in the brain. They thus equate what they are with the brain rather than with any other part of the body, and shrink with instinctive horror from anything which they perceive as a direct interference with the brain. To pierce it with surgical instruments, or to pass an electric current through it, provokes in many people a horror of a quite primitive kind. And, since both these procedures began as crude attempts to use new techniques and were not always successful, the original gut reaction has been overlaid with a rational suspicion that a brain operation may change a man's personality and that electro-convulsive therapy may reduce him to a zombie-like state.

Public anxiety about drugs or medicines is less primitive. But, although the thalidomide tragedies caused great concern about the safety of drugs, a very large number of people regard the pill bottle as one of the everyday appurtenances of twentieth century living. Indeed, for many prisoners, one of the worst deprivations of life behind bars is to be deprived of the drugs which provide a crutch for their inadequate lives. Yet, in the containment of mental illnesses, the accumulating evidence of the use of certain drugs over long periods seems to point to another possible attack on the citadel of an individual's personality, as much to be feared as that produced by the knife or the electric current.

For over two hundred years safeguards against the exploitation of people whose minds are disturbed have been built into the law. Mostly, they are concerned with ensuring humane conditions in hospitals, the protection of patients' property, and assurances that sane men are not locked away as insane. Only since technology has brought the possibility of "cure" has there been discussion of the uses to which treatment may be put, and particularly of its use for patients held against their will. It was this which brought the Butler Committee into existence, whose Report [1] provoked the response of a White Paper [2]. Neither document, however, considered the use of treatment outside the National Health Service.

There has been no organised discussion of the use of the new psychiatric techniques in prisons, and no safeguards have yet been proposed. Nevertheless, it is known that many prisoners suffer from mental disorders, some of which are still barely understood. What is more, prisoners and patients who may be held without limit of time in Special Hospitals such as Broadmoor and Rampton are vulnerable to offers of treatment, whether established or experimental, which may seem to them to offer the possibility of release. And keeping people in prison for long periods costs much public money, and can by itself lead to irreversible deterioration of their personalities — without necessarily deterring or reforming them.

Patients and prisoners alike may be in a position where their ability to understand fully the nature of the treatments they are offered is impaired: the patient because his illness makes it impossible for him to appreciate the hazards of a particular treatment, the prisoner because his desire to be free may obscure his judgement of the consequences of the treatment for him.

In the present state of knowledge and practice there are so many uncertainties that public anxiety is understandable. To assess how far that anxiety is justified, one needs to know what the new techniques can already achieve, and in what ways they are likely to become improved and refined in the foreseeable future; and to consider both how deviant behaviour is currently dealt with — whether in prisons, hospitals, homes or hostels — and what problems it presents for those who serve these institutions. Finally, one must see what safeguards already exist, and whether and how they could be improved.

All that is the theme, and the order, of this Report.

We have been greatly helped by being able to discuss these problems with a number of people who have had direct experience of them, and to whom we are most grateful for the time they have given us, namely:

Dr. Megan Bull	Governor, Holloway Prison.
Dr. Murray Cox	Consultant Psychotherapist, Broadmoor Hospital.
Professor Michael Gelder	Department of Psychiatry, University of Oxford.
Professor Sir Denis Hill	then Professor of Psychiatry, Institute of Psychiatry, London.
Dr. James Orr	Director, Home Office Prison Medical Services.
Mr. Peter Schurr	Neurosurgeon, The Neurosurgical Unit of Guy's, Maudsley, and Kings Hospitals, London.

References

1. Report of the Committee on Mentally Abnormal Offenders, HMSO, 1975, Cmnd. 6244.
2. Review of the Mental Health Act 1959, HMSO, 1978, Cmnd 7320.

2

Techniques of Treatment

2.1. Introduction

Human beings have always tried to control each other's behaviour, sometimes for good reasons, sometimes for bad. Doctors, as their knowledge has increased, have largely been looked up to as benevolent parents, doing what they think best for their patients who have trustingly turned to them.

Psychiatric patients in particular have a long tradition of control by medical men: the asylums of the 19th century, with their orderly regimes for a life of incarceration, were controlled by a Medical Superintendent. But with the scientific advances of the last fifty years it has become possible to effect a lasting influence on men's minds by treating them in the sense understood by the man in the street when he goes to the doctor for the relief of some physical ailment: that is by the administration of drugs, by operations or by expert counselling. But, as happens in all branches of medicine where new techniques become available, some of the benefits are accompanied by unpleasant side-effects, and much remains to be learnt about countering the disadvantages of the new knowledge.

The techniques of treatment most widely used fall into two broad categories: the so-called "physical" treatments — drugs, electro-convulsive therapy and psychosurgery — and the so-called "psychological" treatments — behavioural therapy and psychotherapy. Treatments in the first group are always prescribed by medically qualified people and administered either by themselves or by other professional people authorised by them. Treatments in the second group may be given by doctors. but may also be given by psychologists, lay analysts and counsellors without any medical (or sometimes any other) qualification.

This chapter briefly reviews the various techniques, outlines the methods available in each instance, and looks to future developments. Although the new treatments can undoubtedly be beneficial, this chapter deliberately points to some of the hazards, reversible or not, which have to be weighed in the balance before a treatment is prescribed.

A. Physical Treatments

2.2 Psychotropic Drugs

These are drugs which alter mood and behaviour in various ways. Some alter the function of the mind in a normal person, others are primarily effective in the treatment of mental disorder. They can be divided into a number of distinct groups and we deal with them in order of increasing importance to our problem.

2.3 Hypnotics and Tranquillizers

Hypnotics are sleeping tablets. Tranquillizers, as their name implies, act as sedatives: that is, they calm, but are less inclined than hypnotics to make people drowsy.

The earliest medicaments of this kind were the bromides, chloral and paraldehyde. But, in this century, the main hypnotics and tranquillizers have been the barbiturates such as phenobarbitone (Luminal), butobarbitone (Soneryl), and quinalbarbitone (Seconal). Because of their limited effectiveness, and because of the danger of patients taking overdoses, they are now much less used and have been largely replaced by drugs such as diazepam (Valium) and chlordiazepoxide (Librium), members of a chemical class of drugs called the benzodiazepines.

These drugs are used to relieve symptoms of anxiety, insomnia, tension and muscle spasm, and so common have they become that a recent survey has shown that about 20 per cent of women in the general population now use such drugs at some time in the course of a year. Women use drugs more than men, who tend to turn to tobacco or alcohol to relieve the same symptoms.[1]

The side-effects of the benzodiazepines and other tranquillizers are usually sleepiness and the slowing of thought. Paradoxically, however, stimulant effects have been seen in some patients when their anxiety is lifted. They may become hostile or openly aggressive, rather as some people do under the influence of alcohol.[2]

2.4 Antidepressants

This is a group of drugs used to relieve depression, comprising mainly amitryptiline (Tryptizol) and imipramine (Tofranil). The side-effects are sometimes unpleasant but rarely dangerous or irreversible.

2.5 Lithium Carbonate

This substance has been widely and successfully used to stabilise patients with manic-depressive illnesses which are characterised by swings of mood from euphoria to depression.

It has adverse effects, both short and long-term. In the short term there can be toxic effects if body levels are excessive, when the functions of heart, brain and kidneys are all impaired. In the long term, after months or years of use, kidneys may be irreparably damaged.

2.6 Antipsychotics

These drugs are also known as neuroleptics or major tranquillizers. Of 20 such drugs currently available in the United Kingdom, the most popular remains chlorpromazine (Largactil), the first to be introduced. Trifluoperazine (Stelazine), thioridazine (Melleril) and haloperidol (Haldol) are also widely used. Injections into muscles of long-acting 'depot' preparations — fluphenazine decanoate (Modecate), and flupenthixol decanoate (Depixol) — are also convenient and popular. Antipsychotic drugs have a wide range of clinical uses:

1. They exert a quietening effect on severely disturbed patients.
2. They diminish certain special features of psychotic illness such as hallucinations and delusions. They are the main treatment for schizophrenia, especially in its acute form.
3. They prevent or postpone relapses in chronic schizophrenic illnesses.

Despite their undoubted advantages, these drugs have sometimes been dismissed as "chemical straitjackets", and there is some substance in that accusation. Their action is primarily to combat symptoms rather than to alter the mechanism underlying a particular condition. Used as major tranquillizers, they are often administered to very disturbed patients who are hostile, aggressive and otherwise uncontrollable. In such situations, the patient may be in a condition of clouded consciousness, as if he were delirious. In many cases he is incapable of understanding what is happening to him and may actively resist treatment.

The side-effects of antipsychotic drugs severely limit their usefulness. Common among them are dry mouth, blurred vision, constipation, dizziness, falls in blood pressure and a pounding heart. Particularly unpleasant are the effects on voluntary movement which becomes increasingly difficult; the patient's expression becomes fixed and mask-like; his hands tremble. (The clinical picture mimics that of Parkinsonism, a degenerative neurological disease sometimes called paralysis agitans). In other patients the drug may induce painful muscular spasms or severe restlessness. Happily all these effects disappear when the drug is discontinued or the dosage lowered.

A much more worrying side-effect is the condition known as tardive dyskinesia, characterised by repetitive involuntary movements of a tremulous, twitching or writhing nature involving the mouth, lips, tongue, trunk and limbs. In mild degrees it is unsightly and upsetting. In more severe degrees it interferes with eating and breathing. The condition is sometimes irreversible. It may come on months or years after antipsychotic medication is started — hence its name. It may sometimes start when treatment ceases and probably reflects semi-permanent changes in nerve cells in the brain which control muscular activity. Many treatments have been tried to lessen these involuntary movements but none has any lasting effect.

Tardive dyskinesia is commonest in the elderly but is not unknown in children. After about 10 years of continuous treatment, 25-50% of schizophrenic patients display the condition, though it is mild in most cases.

2.7 Drugs to Control Sexual Behaviour

Antipsychotic drugs have been used to decrease sexual drive as part of a general tranquillizing action, but hormones and anti-hormones are more selective in altering sexual drive.

Female sex hormones, administered to men, have a castration-like effect, diminishing sex drive and impairing sexual performance. Another approach is a drug such as cyproterone (an anti-androgen), which prevents the actions of male sex hormones in the brain and body. Again sex drive is lessened.

These treatments have been used for many years in patients convicted of sexual offences[3], but scientific evaluations have been few.

The side effects of these treatments are widespread. The major one is breast enlargement, which is often irreversible, necessitating removal of the breasts. The treatments cannot be used in physically immature young men, as they may stop bone growth prematurely.

2.8 Electro-Convulsive Therapy (ECT)

This treatment involves the brief passage of an electric current through the brain to induce an epileptic fit. The fit is modified because the patient is fully anaesthetised, and his muscles are completely relaxed. How the treatment works cannot be firmly established because direct studies cannot be carried out on human brain tissue. But evidence from animal studies suggests that biochemical changes take place in the brain which are important in the relief of some forms of mental illness.

The few scientifically controlled clinical trials of ECT which have taken place suggest that it is an effective treatment for severely depressed patients, three quarters or more recovering completely after 4-8 applications over 3-4 weeks. Its usefulness in other conditions is not so well established.

The main adverse effect of the treatment is memory impairment, but this is difficult to evaluate, as depressive illness may itself impair concentration and memory. It has indeed recently been found that the memories of patients who have received a single course of 8 applications show no evidence of impairment.

Death from ECT is rare: the risk is of the same order as that from dental procedures requiring an anaesthetic. This has to be set against the very real risk of suicide in deeply depressed patients. In addition, the risk of death from other causes, such as heart attacks, is increased in untreated depressives.

ECT has undoubtedly been used too enthusiastically in some patients who have had many treatments in an attempt to control psychotic behaviour, and also to treat some patients who were not psychotic. Its use should be regarded as experimental in conditions other than severe depression and for some forms of schizophrenia and mania. On balance it is a very useful treatment for carefully selected patients, but a course of treatment should not normally exceed 12 applications and may succeed with far fewer.

2.9 Psychosurgery

Psychosurgery is a general term for several neurological procedures which aim to modify feelings or behaviour by cutting or destroying parts of the brain. The structure and function of the various parts of the brain are ill-understood, but there are some, like the frontal lobes, which seem to be concerned with emotions and with self-control. The techniques covered by the term psychosurgery include various means of partially disconnecting the frontal lobes from the rest of the brain (prefrontal leucotomies), and the removal of significant parts of the limbic system such as the cingulus or the amygdala (amygdalectomy). Sometimes the operations are carried out for purely functional disorders (such as severe depression, intense anxiety, crippling phobias, marked obsessionality with rituals and compulsions). At other times, operations (though still partly designed to relieve functional symptoms), are also aimed at interrupting brain circuits which are producing abnormal electrical discharges and epileptic fits; whole lobes of the brain are sometimes removed to this end.

Great controversy has surrounded psychosurgery, and this has to be related to its history. The early leucotomy operations were crude cuts across the frontal lobes of the brain, operations which often left the patient without initiative or self-control and suffering from epileptic fits. Modern techniques are more sophisticated and precise, but they are still empirical in that brain connections and functions are not fully understood.

Amygdalectomy was introduced as a means of treating intractable epilepsy. In some patients it also seemed to reduce aggression. It has therefore been used on occasions as a means of reducing aggression in patients without epilepsy. Such a procedure is rare and remains unproven.

There are 44 neurological units in the British Isles where brain operations are performed. During the period 1974-6 they were responsible for 431 operations for functional mental illness — a yearly rate of

3.4 operations per million of the adult population over the age of 15. Four units did two-thirds of the operations; only 8% had operations for conditions involving repeated violence.[4]

Surgery of this kind, if it is carried out at all, should only be undertaken in specialised centres, and only after every other possibility of help has been exhausted. Many psychiatrists feel that psychosurgery should never be carried out on prisoners, since their judgement is bound to be affected by the very fact of their confinement.

B. Psychological Treatments

2.10 Behaviour Therapy

Treatments under this heading have evolved from psychological studies of animal and human behaviour. Underlying the treatment is the belief that some abnormal behaviour results not from factors within the body, but from factors in the patient's environment.

Many therapists (who describe their subjects as "clients" rather than "patients") use "operant" methods derived from animal studies of learning processes in rats and pigeons. Almost all of these make use of "reinforcement techniques" — a reinforcer being defined as "any manipulation which increases or maintains the pattern of behaviour or interest". An example of such a method is the "token economy" where chronic schizophrenic patients are awarded tokens when they successfully complete a desired piece of behaviour, such as dressing themselves. The tokens can then be used to purchase additional privileges.

Techniques using what are known as "negative reinforcers" can similarly be devised to reduce undesirable behaviour. Negative reinforcers are a form of punishment, in that a patient has to be discouraged from persisting with unacceptable behaviour. It is difficult to define what are positive and negative reinforcers, for one man's meat is another man's poison. A masochist may enjoy electric shocks, and Smarties are not every child's idea of heaven.

In a more extreme form, negative reinforcement becomes "aversion therapy". There, the patient is allowed to carry out the unwanted act and is then punished for it. For example, the alcoholic is given free access to his bottle of gin in conditions which remind him of his local pub, but afterwards he is given an injection which makes him feel sick. Gradually he comes to associate the feeling of sickness with the bottle and so abjures it. This technique is not very successful, perhaps because of its artificiality.

Other widely used treatments are mainly cognitive, making use of the patient's thought. The obsessional ruminator is encouraged to stop thinking about his obsessions by focussing on something else; the phobic is trained to contemplate the object or the situation which he fears, first in imagination and next in reality, thereby gradually coming to terms with his fears. In the same way, the gauche are taught social skills; the obsessional, terrified of contamination, are shown that dirt has no magical powers of harm.

2.11 Psychotherapy

Psychotherapy is a generic term covering a wide range of interactive verbal techniques which seek to modify patients' attitudes, feelings, beliefs and behaviour. Some would include behaviour therapy among the psychotherapies, but the techniques mentioned here differ from behaviour therapy in being more concerned with personality change. Behaviour therapy is more narrowly concerned with symptom relief and the modification of particular elements of behaviour. Most psychotherapies are derived, at least in part, from psychoanalytic theory.

2.12 Psychoanalysis

Psychoanalysis was invented by Sigmund Freud in the 1890s. It is still the most formal and time-consuming of all methods of psychotherapy, and can be considered the forerunner of many of the modern briefer techniques. Several schools of psychoanalysis exist. All require frequent lengthy individual sessions (perhaps one hour, three to five times a week), but they use different methods. In free association, the patient reports his thoughts without reservation. These are then interpreted, that is they are given meaning according to their context and according to that school's psychoanalytic theory.

In most forms of individual psychotherapy derived from psychoanalysis today it is assumed that neurotic disorders are the consequence of disturbances and distortions in the patient's relations with other people during the course of his development. Analysis of the transference — that is, of the patient's attitudes and feelings towards the analyst — therefore becomes an essential part of the treatment. It is assumed that if the patient can learn to relate to the analyst in a more normal and rational manner, he will carry this capacity to make good relationships outside the analytic setting and be able to make more fruitful and better relationships with people in ordinary life.

Underlying most forms of psychotherapy, and especially psychoanalysis, are important psychological concepts such as psychic determinism. This sees psychological significance in all human behaviour, including speech, so that casual remarks, slips of the tongue, accidents etc, are understood in terms of a person's needs, motivations, wishes, including their unconscious aspects.

The doctrine of the "unconscious" is the second major concept. It is postulated that parts of mental life are normally inaccessible to conscious recall, even though such mental life is having an effect on consciousness and behaviour. The idea that parts of mental life could be unconscious and yet have an influence on conscious behaviour was current long before Freud; but it was he who formulated the notion that making conscious what had been unconscious was a major part of the psychoanalytic endeavour.

The third major concept of psychoanalysis overlaps with learning theory in that it assumes that neurotic symptoms and maladaptive behavioural patterns are the result of learning and previous experience. There has been a good deal of argument about Freud's concept of psychic energy and his structural division of the mind into id, ego and superego. Freud's was essentially a biological theory and some later analysts have tried to re-state it in sociological and environmental terms. The various analytical schools, such as those of Melanie Klein, C.G. Jung and Alfred Adler, all owe a debt to Freud's way of thinking, but have diverged in one way or another from some of his basic assumptions.

2.13 Group Therapy

Group therapy is any form of psychotherapy in which more than one patient is treated at a time. It developed originally for economic reasons: one therapist could analyse or treat several patients simultaneously. However, group treatments have advantages and disadvantages of their own. Transference reactions develop between group members, as well as between the therapist and each member. It is much harder for the therapist to impose a particular system or theory on the group. A patient can work through several relationship problems simultaneously.

2.14 Therapeutic Communities

The development of therapeutic communities can largely be traced back to war-time experiments. They involve regular group meetings between patients and therapists to discuss personal problems, as well as devolution of decision-making, as far as possible, to staff of all grades, and especially to patients.

Most psychiatric hospitals now include some elements of this process, but particularly good examples of therapeutic communities have been developed for the treatment of patients and offenders with behaviour disorders. Two of the best known centres are the Henderson Hospital and Grendon Prison.

2.15 Encounter Groups

Early psychotherapy concerned itself with verbal activity alone. In recent years, bodily contact has been encouraged as part of group psychotherapeutic activity. The aim of such encounter groups is to increase physical as well as emotional sensitivity to others, and to overcome some of the physical inhibitions of which patients frequently complain.

2.16 Psychodrama

This refers to a specialised form of group treatment in which the sessions are partially structured to give each patient a role, relevant to his own problems, which he can then act, in relation to other patients acting their problem roles. It is believed that by this process individuals gain new understanding of their own difficulties, and learn new ways of surmounting them.

2.17 Counselling

Counselling often means advice with educational difficulties, or job problems, or marriage adjustment. However, personal counselling usually involves some kind of psychotherapeutic relationship, and the resolution of that relationship is part of the counselling process.

In the most elaborate school of counselling (as established by Rogers in America), great emphasis is put on the distance between the current self-image and the ideal self of the client, while the therapist is enjoined to be utterly genuine and transparent when conducting his treatment, to value the client warmly as an important separate individual, and take great pains to see the world as the client does.

2.18 Future Developments

In the foreseeable future it will probably be possible to develop drugs to treat mental disorders, which will not have the unpleasant side-effects we have noted at the beginning of this chapter. Basic science is developing at such a rate that our knowledge of the brain mechanisms involved in such conditions is increasing rapidly and eventually more specific drugs may become available. For example, it might conceivably be possible to have a drug specifically to treat aggression, or to arrest the intellectual decay of old age. But it is unlikely that highly specific drugs will be developed for some time. Spectres of controlling whole populations by means of drugs added to the drinking-water remain in the sphere of science fiction.

Future drugs for the control of sexual behaviour will probably centre on increasing the selective actions of the anti-androgens, so that sexual drives are lessened without influencing other bodily tissues. Much basic work is being carried out into the brain mechanisms underlying sexual behaviour, so that drugs with novel modes of action may become feasible. It is improbable, however, that we are very near to the production of a drug which could alter the direction, rather than the magnitude, of the sex-drive. Here behavioural techniques are likely to remain more appropriate.

It looks as though we are more likely over the course of the next decades to see small improvements in what we have, rather than major innovations. But the history of psychotropic drugs is one of discovery by accident rather than by directed experiment, and there may well be fortunate accidents of this kind which might herald changes at present impossible to foresee. One which is already on the horizon is the possibility of a drug which could influence not the developed brain, but the way in which the brain develops. It may soon be possible to administer drugs to young animals and humans which will modify the levels of aggression or anxiety as the brain develops.

Electro-convulsive therapy will probably be refined so that more localised currents can be passed across the head, thus avoiding some of the side-effects of present methods. Many centres already use electro-convulsive shocks to one side of the head only with this very object, but it is unlikely that much further localisation could be achieved in this way without the surgical insertion of electrodes. The implanting of electrodes has been carried out in a few studies, but again the behaviour modifications induced were much less specific than might have been expected.

Future developments in psychosurgery are likely to be slow. There is no evidence that one area of the brain alone is concerned with aggression. The balance of the brain's functional activity is so important that the ability to intervene with highly specific brain lesions is not very likely to be productive. Gross symptomatic improvement may be effected, and gross interference with general behavioural levels may be possible, but it is unlikely that specific changes can be produced.

It is difficult to foresee major advances in behaviour therapy. As a realistic appraisal of its potential has been attained there is already some disillusionment with its benefits. It may be that it will in future be combined with other approaches — psychotherapy and drug treatment in particular — to maximise its potential.

Psychotherapy remains controversial, and it is difficult to see how the more intensive analytical techniques could be much further developed. Rather it is likely that the standard techniques will move more and more towards counselling and group therapy.

References

1. Balter, M.B., Levine, J. and Mannheimer, D.I. (1974) "Cross-national study of the extent of anti-anxiety/sedative drug use". *New England Journal of Medicine*, *290*, 767-774.
2. Gaind, R.N. and Jacoby, R. (1978) "Benzodiazepines causing aggression". Gaind, R.N. and Hudson, B.L. (Eds) *Current Themes in Psychiatry*. London, pp. 371-379.
3. See, for example, a report in the *Daily Telegraph* for April 25, 1979, according to which a convicted child molester at the Central Criminal Court was offered this treatment as an alternative to a long term of imprisonment.

4. Barraclough, B.M., and Mitchell-Heggs, N.A. (1978) "Use of neurosurgery for psychological disorder in British Isles during 1974-6"; *British Medical Journal 2*, 1591-3.

3

Places of Confinement

Since the techniques described in the last Chapter all relate to and affect states of mind or conduct, many are employed in the psychiatric hospitals and prisons. In recent years there has been public disquiet that all is not well in either.

True, the psychiatric hospitals are more open than they have ever been. True, the new techniques of treatment have greatly shortened the average length of each hospital stay. But a good many people are still there against their will and, though it has not been part of our task to inquire into the truth of allegations against certain hospitals, we have read a number of well-documented reports which would seem to support some of them.

As to the prisons, their general overcrowding is public knowledge, and so is the grumbling discontent of the prison officers whose task it is to care for the prisoners. Conditions in prisons are far less open to public scrutiny than those in psychiatric hospitals; the Official Secrets Act can be used, rightly or wrongly, to block free access to the press, which has nonetheless been quick to seize on articles in prison journals which give cause for alarm.

In this and subsequent chapters, we have confined ourselves to conditions as they apply to England and Wales, and have not attempted to cover the differences in Scottish or Northern Irish law, practice, or terminology. Had we done so, we would have lengthened the term of our inquiry, and we believe our main conclusions can be applied equally to the situation north of the Border or west of the Irish Channel.

3.1 The Psychiatric Hospitals

Psychiatric Hospitals are part of the National Health Service. In England they are in the ultimate charge of the Secretary of State for Social Services; in Wales they are in the charge of the Secretary of State for Wales. The country is divided into Regions, and the Health Authorities controlling them are appointed by the Secretary of State and are responsible for the general conduct of the hospitals and the well-being of the patients.

As a matter of professional practice, psychiatrists tend to operate on a catchment-area basis, deciding among themselves for which localities they will be responsible. Most people in a catchment area would find it difficult to arrange for a different psychiatric service or opinion if they were dissatisfied with the service provided. They might have the option of persuading their general practitioner to refer them to a teaching hospital where catchment areas are not rigorously applied, but such opportunities will only fall to a small number of patients.

A patient, therefore, who needs to go to hospital for a mental illness will normally have no choice as to the hospital which will treat him, though in nine cases out of ten he will enter hospital of his own free will — that is, as an informal patient. He will then be as free as he would be in a general hospital to leave when he feels better, although he might be unwise to do so until the doctor in charge of his case agrees that he is fit to go. He will find the doors of the ward open, and his friends and relations will be free, and encouraged, to visit him. There are, however, in most hospitals one or two wards which are locked.

3.2 Compulsory Admission Procedures

Unlike other specialist services, the psychiatric services have the power and the duty to cater for patients who are admitted to hospital involuntarily under the Mental Health Act 1959. Under Sections 25, 26 and 29 of the Act, patients are admitted for shorter or longer periods for observation or for treatment.

The usual procedure for holding a patient against his will is for a certificate to be signed by a relative or social worker and two doctors (one of whom has to be a psychiatrist), and for this certificate to last for a period not exceeding 28 days in the first instance; then for one year, after which it is renewable for a further year; then every two years. The "managers" of the hospital (that is the Health Authority concerned) have to be satisfied at all stages that the patient is appropriately placed.

The psychiatrist has complete authority to reclassify the patient as "informal" at any stage he thinks appropriate. In the case of the small proportion of patients detained for more than 28 days, a relative can bring pressure to bear on a doctor to do so, for he also has the power to have the patient discharged, but he has to give three days' notice of his intention, and the doctor can bar the patient's discharge if he thinks he is likely to act in a manner dangerous to himself or other people.

In acute emergencies, the police, if they find someone "who appears to be suffering from mental disorder" and "think him to be in immediate need of care or control", have power (under Section 136 of the Act) to hold him against his will for three days. In such cases the police usually take the sufferer straight to hospital.

However he is admitted, the patient has rights of appeal against his detention, as has his nearest relative. During the first month, the patient can appeal directly to the hospital managers. After that, he can make regular applications to an independent Mental Health Review Tribunal consisting of a lawyer, a psychiatrist and a lay person, which can decide to uphold his appeal and release him immediately.

3.3 Mentally Abnormal Offenders

Arrangements are slightly different for the mentally abnormal offender who has been dealt with in a court of law. Under Section 60, adult offenders over 21 who suffer from personality disorders, or from only a moderate degree of intellectual impairment, can be included under the longer-term compulsory arrangements, and in their case relatives are not involved or consulted. With the agreement of the managers, a patient can be admitted to hospital, if the court deems it appropriate, and if two psychiatrists are willing to sign a certificate.

Once he is admitted, the arrangements are very similar to those already outlined, in that the consultant psychiatrist in charge of the case has power to discharge the patient at any time, and the patient has a right to appeal to the Mental Health Review Tribunal.

Occasionally, under Section 65, a judge may make a "restriction order" which removes the power of discharge from the consultant psychiatrist and the Mental Health Review Tribunal and vests it in the Home Secretary, who may refer such a case to a Tribunal for their advice, but is not bound to accept it. The criteria for discharge in these cases are not purely medical, but are concerned with the protection of the public.

3.4 Special Hospitals

There are four Special Hospitals for England and Wales: Broadmoor, Rampton, Moss Side and Park Lane. These are run directly by the Department of Health and Social Security. They are "special" in that they are security hospitals, patients being held under lock and key. At one point in their history they were, like the prisons, run by the Home Office and they still preserve some historical connections with that period: their nurses, although fully trained, tend to belong to the Prison Officers' Association, and many of them wear blue uniforms like prison officers.

Special Hospital beds are in great demand, and can only be obtained from the Department of Health and Social Security. They are sought only when a patient cannot be adequately managed in a conventional psychiatric hospital and nursing in conditions of maximum security is unavoidable. Not surprisingly, most of the patients in the Special

Hospitals are those who have come to the notice of the courts.

They are usually detained under Section 60, but many of them have a Section 65 restriction order added, so that they can only be discharged with the approval of the Home Secretary. Their confinement is therefore not for a fixed term as it would be in prison.

3.5 Regional Medium Security Units

Because of the pressure on the Special Hospitals, and the difficulty of providing a structured environment within ordinary psychiatric hospitals, there has been pressure on the Regions to provide at least a few "medium security" beds. These would be for patients who require management in a structured environment, who are unsuitable for the complete freedom of an open ward, but who do not need the maximum security of a Special Hospital. Roughly 1,000 such beds are planned for the whole country, but most Regions have not yet been able to establish even interim arrangements along these lines, although the necessary funds have been made available to them.

3.6 Prisons

Prisons are the responsibility of the Home Secretary. Unlike his colleague the Secretary of State for Social Services, he does not depute his responsibility to Regional Boards, but exercises it directly through his Department, the Home Office. Most prisons have Boards of Visitors who are required to oversee the needs of prisoners in a number of ways and who are appointed by the Home Secretary, but they have no administrative responsibilities for the way in which a prison is run.

3.7 The Prison Medical Service

The Home Office operates a special medical service for the prisons which is not part of the National Health Service, though controversy has raged for a number of years as to whether it should be. At present the full-time service is very much below establishment, and it is questionable whether it is able to attract enough top quality doctors. It is concentrated in the larger prisons which have hospital facilities and provide medical reports to the Courts. The Medical Director of the Service is based at the Home Office, which also employs a large number of general practitioners on a part-time basis, as well as visiting psychiatrists and psychotherapists. There are a few joint appointments of consultant forensic psychiatrists working half-time in prisons and half-time in the psychiatric hospitals. Smaller prisons, open prisons, and those where the demand for medical services is considered to be low, may have no full-time medical officer attached, but will depend on part-time local general practitioners for day-to-day services.

Some of the hospitals in larger prisons are reasonably equipped and can offer sophisticated medical and surgical care. Others are little more than sick-bays. One prison (Grendon) is a psychiatric prison and therapeutic community for personality-disordered and neurotic prisoners, with a Governor who is a doctor.

Specialist services are obtained by inviting NHS consultants to examine and treat in prison any prisoner who has problems beyond the scope of normal prison care. Some are transferred into NHS hospitals on a temporary basis for medical, surgical or psychiatric care. That, at least, is the theory, but it rarely becomes fact in the case of severe psychiatric illness. Section 72 of the Mental Health Act makes it possible to transfer a prisoner with such an illness to a psychiatric hospital, but in recent years this has proved increasingly difficult because of the reluctance of hospitals to accept such patients.

The prison medical officer is responsible for advising the Governor of the prison on all matters relating to the health of the prisoners. Although he has complete clinical freedom in his everyday practice, he comes under the guidance of senior doctors at the Home Office for the administration of his department within the policy of his particular prison.

Some medical officers have specialist experience in psychiatry, and within the prison setting provide many of the treatments familiar in the specialist hospitals, including psychotherapy, psychotropic drugs and ECT. To assist them they have hospital officers, who are selected from among the prison officers and given a short period of nursing training. These are not qualified nurses, but they are trained in a number of procedures such as the giving of injections under the direct supervision of a doctor.

3.8 Pressures in Hospitals

Of the many thousands of patients who pass through psychiatric hospitals during the course of a year, nine out of ten are admitted as informal patients. At any one time, about 22,000 people are detained against their will, of whom all but 500 will be classified as suffering from mental illness. (The 500 are those classified as "severely subnormal"). Most patients stay only a short time — about six weeks — but there are still a great many who are beyond the reach of treatments so far available. Among these patients are many old people whose need is for asylum and understanding care.

To look after patients who may be irrational, aggressive, unpredictable, incontinent or cunning, or exhibit a combination of all these characteristics, demands quite exceptional patience and calm and a high degree of skill. But many hospitals are badly understaffed, particularly on the long-stay wards, and it is easy to see how overwork and exasperation can bring about a crisis in which tempers fray, and conformity with hospital regimes may sometimes be obtained by means which would not be used if staffing were adequate to the demands of the job.

What is true in the ordinary psychiatric hospitals is even more the case in the Special Hospitals where by definition patients present management problems; if they did not they would not be there.

3.9 Pressures in Prisons

Pressures in prisons are certainly no less. In 1979 the average daily prison population reached a record level of 42,220. As a consequence of gross overcrowding, the number of prisoners sharing cells rose to 16,585 and, of these, as many as 4,833 were sleeping three to a cell, and this in prison buildings which are already gravely sub-standard. The 1978 Report of the work of the Prison Department admitted that of the 56 prisons which date from before 1930, only 10 are in good condition, 39 are fair and 7 are poor. One Governor said of his prisoners and staff that they were living and suffering in Dickensian conditions, and another was reported as saying that there was nothing wrong with his prison which the expenditure of several million pounds would not put right. Successive governments have shrugged off these lamentable facts, and money for the prison service remains a low political priority.

The result for the prisoners is that they are often confined to their cells for excessive periods. Morale and discipline deteriorate along a spiral path: detention in cells leads to boredom and the accumulation of pent-up energies; violence, never far below the surface, flares and still longer periods in the cells follow. The effect of these conditions on prisoners and prison officers alike is not hard to imagine.

Add to these unsatisfactory physical conditions the fact that it has been estimated that a third of all sentenced prisoners suffer from psychiatric abnormality, and an explosive situation is bound to result.

3.10 Offenders in the Community

It is against the background of pressure in both hospitals and prisons that we have had to consider the use to which the new technologies now available might be put: it is there that the ethical problems can be seen in their sharpest relief. But pressure to accept treatment may sometimes be exerted by courts in offering an offender alternatives to a prison sentence. He may, for example, be made subject to a probation order with a condition of residence for up to one year in a named probation hostel or rehabilitative unit, after spending a remand period there so that the authorities and he can both assess whether he will benefit from the regime offered. If, after such an order, he cannot or will not conform, he will eventually either abscond or return to court for the order to be varied.

Probation hostels offer no specific medical treatment, though residents may be required to attend the local hospital for out-patient medical or psychiatric care. The hostels provide an orderly environment in which offenders can live and from which they can go out to work. Counselling and group discussion may form part of the règime: intensive psychotherapy generally does not.

If, however, the offender has specific drug or alcohol problems, he may have a condition of residence in a rehabilitative unit inserted into his probation order. These units, often with charitable status, are independently run and managed. Their management committees (including consultant psychiatrists, psychotherapists, probation officers and representatives of the Area Health Authority), have a minimal influence on the actual regime within the unit, which is usually set up by someone with a mission which may be psychotherapeutic, behaviourist or religious in emphasis, The support staff are typically "graduates" of the regime — themselves reformed addicts. Treatment is intensive, conducted within the closed community where very strong pressures may be exerted on inmates, and unusual forms of coercion sometimes used to persuade them to conform to the process.

Children in the care of local authorities are liable to find themselves placed in a variety of establishments. As with units treating drug and alcohol abuse, special homes which treat disturbed juveniles may operate in a variety of ways, ranging from the psychotherapeutic to the purely behavioural.

In all the situations described in this chapter, patients and persons confined for their own good or for the good of society might benefit from the new technologies and are certainly at risk from their dangers. In the next chapters we describe the existing safeguards which protect them.

4 Ethical Safeguards

All sorts of problems confront professional workers in hospitals, prisons, hostels or children's homes who have to deal with difficult residents. Again and again they are called upon to resolve difficult ethical questions.

4.1 Professional Ethics

To illustrate the problem we take the medical profession as the example. It is a basic part of the ethics of the medical profession that treatment can only be given to a patient after he has given his informed and free consent. (We discuss the wider implications of the need for consent in Chapter 5). In an emergency, where the patient's life or safety is in jeopardy, prior consent may be dispensed with at the discretion of the medical practitioner, but treatment may not be given against the clear wishes of a sane patient who is conscious and declines to be treated. (It is not, for example, unknown for a Jehovah's Witness, even in the face of death, to refuse a blood transfusion.) Exceptions to this rule include minors and unconscious patients, when nearest relatives or legal guardians are consulted, and emergencies in which the patient's express wishes cannot be ascertained.

Occasionally patients detained under the Mental Health Act are treated despite their objection, sometimes after a second psychiatric opinion has been sought, and sometimes after relatives or guardians have been consulted. The guiding principle for such compulsory treatment is that it is wrong to deprive a patient of treatment because a mental abnormality interferes with his judgement.

There is an exception to this rule. Prison doctors — though, at least in theory, in the same position as family doctors — are subject to some constraints. They may impose compulsory treatment on a mentally disturbed prisoner *in an emergency* if it will prevent a serious deterioration in his condition, or save his life, or prevent his behaving violently and being a danger to himself or other people. (In this the policy of the Home Office follows the recommendations of the Butler Committee which we discuss in Chapter 5). But prisons are not psychiatric hospitals, and the provisions of the Mental Health Act do not apply there. When, therefore, a prisoner appears to need compulsory treatment but does not constitute an emergency, the prison doctor's remedy is to sign a Section 72 order under the Mental Health Act , and seek the consent of the Home Secretary to remove him to a psychiatric hospital for treatment. He cannot be compulsorily treated in these circumstances in prison.

But situations can arise where prisoners are so ill psychiatrically that they ought to be treated but, because there are difficulties about their transfer to psychiatric hospitals (see Section 3.7), they remain in prison without appropriate treatment — a loss of a basic right to treatment which Parliament certainly never intended.

Ethical questions arise when doctors are called to deal with "emergencies" wherever they occur. Is the emergency a crisis in the individual's medical condition? Or is it one of management? The distinction is often a fine one and can present a crisis of conscience for the professional.[1]

4.2 Problems of Prison Discipline

The ethical problem for a prison Governor in these situations is different. He is concerned with achieving the best balance between conflicting objectives. He has responsibilities to the prisoners, individually and collectively: to maintain their physical well-being and to see that they are helped and not damaged by their stay in prison — under present conditions an almost impossible ideal. He must ensure that they do each other no harm. (Many of them are, indeed, segregated at their own request, or on the Governor's orders for their own protection.)

But he has other responsibilities too towards the prison staff. Relaxed conditions which may help a prisoner to gain self-respect, are not necessarily those most helpful to the staff for maintaining good order, especially when staffs are short-handed. Highly authoritarian regimes are easiest to operate, and it is often these which provide the flashpoint of disturbance. So when the Governor calls on his medical officer for advice he must often be tempted to wish for "control by the needle", and for some good reason for medical intervention. And who can blame him, when his concern is for the greatest good for the greatest number? Who can blame him too, when to place a man in a body belt is the only alternative means of containing his behaviour?

4.3 Treatment Dilemmas

The more usual dilemmas faced by professional people in the treatment of disturbed behaviour is to know what treatment to choose. If, after a period, a doctor makes use of the more potent drugs described in Chapter 2, does he have a duty to explain to the patient the side-effects to which he may be subject — particularly when, if he does not follow this particular treatment, his life is likely to be spent in hospital, and he will be denied the measure of independent life in the community which the drug could give him? If he offers, for example, hormone treatment to prisoners convicted of sexual acts against children, how does the doctor balance the physical risk to his patient against the possible benefit he may derive from a decreased sex-drive, particularly when firm data about the benefits and drawbacks of the oestrogens and anti-androgens are sparse? How long should he resist a patient's antipathy to ECT when the risk of suicide is high and this is the only treatment to which a particular patient is known to respond?

For the practitioners of behavioural and psychotherapeutic techniques there are other ethical problems. Many behaviour therapists draw up a treatment "contract" with their patient, setting out the aims and methods of treatment, but operant techniques which involve penalties or the withdrawal of privileges pose the question "what is it reasonable to withold?" In a way the ethical problem here is less with prisoners than with patients: the former are already so restricted, having lost most of their civil rights, that whole batteries of privileges could be devised as positive reinforcers. But for patients, a high standard of care should be the minimum, so that additional rewards may be less obvious. A cigarette is a powerful reward to a prisoner, but not to a patient who has tobacco freely available in the hospital shop. Negative reinforcers pose even more thorny problems, for if they are too powerful they may become inhuman or infringe basic rights.

The dangers of psychotherapy are less obvious, but they exist. For some patients the psychotherapeutic process is too stressful, and they become much worse, sometimes lapsing into severe mental illness. Others can develop severe depression: suicides in the middle of psychotherapy are by no means unknown. Those forms of treatment which encourage a patient to "act out" (that is, to act on neurotic impulses in real life and not to bottle them up), may involve patients in anti-social or even dangerous behaviour. The transference between therapist and patient is regarded by many therapists as a new mini-neurosis in itself; if it is unsatisfactorily resolved, or if the therapist has to withdraw or dies, the patient may be left with extra symptoms or may be precipitated into severe illness.

A further problem of psychotherapy is the lack of scientific data about its indications, contra-indications, efficacy, and the matching of type of treatment to type of problem. In these circumstances of ignorance, emphasis is necessarily placed upon personal judgement and opinion. While many patients say they have benefited, improvement cannot be readily quantified. Again, there are special considerations relating to consent. Psychotherapy is unlikely to succeed unless the patient wishes to be helped in this way, and can understand something of the nature of the treatment involved, and decide whether he will have it or not. But it is debatable how far a patient can really understand in advance what the development of transference means. Furthermore, the constraints of the transference are such that, before it is resolved, it would either be impossible or very unwise for the patient to leave treatment. A patient may therefore be constrained to continue treatment even when, for other reasons, he would have given it up if he could.

4.4 Professional Safeguards

It is easy to see that even in the hands of highly competent, well-informed, concerned professionals, ethical considerations present complex problems. But in the present state of knowledge, there is also an overriding and chronic problem in the form of unqualified or partly qualified practitioners who overestimate the benefits and underestimate the difficulties, both of the theory and the practice of their discipline.

Any treatment is potentially dangerous. It is possible to use drugs over-enthusiastically: for example, brain development may be stunted by administering certain of them to young children. Operations, including brain operations, could be performed by surgeons without the appropriate skills; all with the best of intentions. It is claimed that some hypnotics and tranquillizers can provoke aggressive outbursts, even in small doses. ECT has no place in the management of behaviour disturbance unless it arises from mental illness. The outcome of psychosurgery, even in the best hands, is not entirely predictable. Whilst children are sent to homes practising token economy regimes (see Section 2.10), there are very few studies which evaluate such treatment.

This welter of ethical problems confronts the psychiatrist day by day. Clearly, therefore, he has to be equipped not only with clinical skills but also with an understanding and training in ethics. It is disturbing to realise that in Britain ethical education, which of course is difficult in that it is not a matter of didactic tuition but the fostering of an approach, is the exception rather than the rule in medical schools and post-graduate courses.

Nevertheless, the medical profession has long devised strict codes of practice and conduct for its members, including machinery for forbidding them to practise if they transgress the rules. The law reinforces this code.

Nurses too have codes of professional practice, are required by law to be registered or enrolled, and are liable to be disciplined for misconduct, which may affect their right to practise.

Psychologists working with "clients" (as they prefer to call them) within the National Health Service are expected to observe the code of practice devised by the British Psychological Society. Transgression of the code could lead to expulsion from the Society, but this would not affect the psychologist's ability to practise; indeed, anyone can set up in private practice as a psychologist. There is as yet no compulsory registration for clinical psychologists, nor any disciplinary body.

Psychotherapists who are also members of another profession which imposes a code of practice will be bound by that code. But there is nothing which requires a practitioner of psychotherapy to belong to any profession, or indeed to fulfil any requirement such as training, before or after setting up in practice. There are many "lay" practitioners who are not bound by any code of professional ethics, in the sense of being exposed to disciplinary proceedings and appropriate sanctions if they behave unethically. Although the best ethical practice among responsible practitioners is at the same level as that of the medical profession, there are currently no means of enforcing it universally. A scheme to provide for such enforcements has been put forward by the principal organisations whose members practise psychotherapy, but this has not so far been put into effect.[2]

The same stage has been reached by the profession of Social Work — a wide term which includes a number of functions for which no educational requirement exists. Standards for professional qualification are however set by the Central Council for Education and Training in Social Work, and about a third of those in the wide class of "social workers" belong to the British Association of Social Workers, which requires its members to observe a defined Code of Ethics with disciplinary sanctions. But expulsion from the British Association of Social Workers carries no prohibition against practice as a social worker. A General Social Work Council to maintain standards of discipline and conduct for the whole profession has been mooted, but is still in the future.

It has to be admitted that no professional codes of conduct, however strict, will guarantee that standards of professional practice remain high. Training in ethical standards needs to be more widespread, so that there is a better general understanding of the ethical codes which are already accepted by many of the professions with which this Report is concerned.

References

1. Similar problems can arise for doctors when the "emergency" is a more public one, such as the detention and interrogation of persons suspected of involvement in a campaign of terrorism. See, on this question, the reports of the Compton and Parker enquiries (references [33] and [34] in the bibliography at the end of this Report).
2. *Statutory Registration of Psychotherapists*, Report of a Professions Joint Working Party, Tavistock Centre (1978).

5 Treatment without Consent: Existing Safeguards

The law is usually seen as a sufficient bulwark against abuse in the ordinary situations of life. Its principles, like those of professional conduct, are often impeccable; it is in their application that difficulties arise. This is particularly so in situations such as those with which we are concerned.

The difficulty is that the law says very little expressly. Because of the variety of situations with which it has to deal, its depth in dealing with any one of them is reduced. The Common Law which governs civil relations and tries to give redress after the event, will generally produce sensible answers for most problems. But even when the sensible answers are built into a system of precedent, they provide no sufficiently detailed code to be a comprehensive guide to conduct, particularly in the type of complex situations to which the techniques which we are now discussing give rise.

The law may not be over-explicit, yet some intelligent forecasts can be made about the way in which the courts would decide in such complex situations. It may be useful to consider some such forecasts in a little detail.

5.1 The Common Law

The law protects a person's physical body with rigour. It says that any form of physical treatment (or restraint) applied without the patient's consent is a trespass or a "battery", a wrong against the person, unless the circumstances are such that his consent may be implied or dispensed with. The wrong is committed even if no damage or injury is caused or likely to be caused, so that the mere threat of a harmless but unauthorised touching can be restrained.

5.2 Dispensing with Consent

Consent may be dispensed with only in cases of "necessity". But when will the law recognise that?

Two different emergencies are usually accepted: the first, in which immediate action is necessary to protect the life or limb of a patient who cannot give his consent: the second, in which the patient is conscious and competent, needs treatment, but refuses his consent although his condition or his behaviour is endangering others.

The judgement required from a doctor or nurse in such cases calls for a nice assessment of all the relevant factors, and may well have to be reached in a moment of great stress or urgency. Essentially, for such crises, the Common Law is "open-ended" and gives little prospective guidance. One cannot predict every type of case in which a court would say that there was justification for acting without consent. While avoiding most of the weighty arguments to which the law has given rise, here are some predictions of the answers. (In considering these, we have chosen the doctor as an example of the professional person, to save too lengthy a discussion.)

In a case where a patient is conscious — after an accident, for example — the outward conflicts are not likely to be acute. Even if the emergency is dramatic and calls for serious action, it may be comparatively easy to discern what has to be done, and there will be no element of dispute with the patient. In fact, the patient's consent can be "presumed". The decision may be easy, but the risks to the interests of the patient may be correspondingly great.

But if the patient is known to be of a religious persuasion which would entirely preclude him, if he were conscious, from giving consent to the proposed treatment, his consent cannot be "presumed". It is doubtful whether in that case a doctor could properly apply treatment, as the law stands. However, if it is uncertain what answer the patient would give if he were conscious, it is likely that a court would hold that the treatment was justified as "reasonably necessary" even if it turned out later that the patient would not in fact have given his consent. Where the condition requiring treatment is the result of the unconscious patient's own suicide attempt, doctors generally assume that he was not sane when he made it, and would consent to resuscitation if he were. In the absence of strong evidence to the contrary, a court would probably uphold such a judgement.

In a case where a conscious patient refuses treatment, a doctor cannot lawfully treat him, assuming that he is satisfied that the patient is competent and appreciates the situation, and that there is no danger to other people. But it may happen in a hospital or a prison that the patient's need for treatment does create a serious danger to other people. The doctor is then faced with a very difficult decision as to the degree of "necessity" involved. It is the nice balance of opposing factors which will decide whether his subsequent action was justified.

There is no doubt that if he acts reasonably to prevent a crime — an assault on other people, for example — he would be justified in law, and suitable action to protect the substantial rights of others to whom the doctor may also owe duties may also be justified. But this merely conceals the balancing process required to determine what ought to be done.

In the light of his knowledge of the circumstances, the doctor (or nurse) will have to weigh:

a) the extent of the danger
b) the existence and nature of any duty owed to the others involved
c) the speed with which the danger requires to be prevented
d) the nature of the patient's condition
e) the effect on and the risks to the patient from carrying out the treatment
f) the nature of the treatment and its general acceptability to society
g) the efficacy of the treatment
h) the reversibility of the treatment
i) the alternative treatments available, either immediately or within the period of the emergency
j) other means available to avert the danger.

However careful he is, the doctor may not know the true facts. If he holds a genuine and reasonable, albeit mistaken, belief about any of the relevant factors, it is likely that a court would exonerate him and hold that he was justified in any reasonable action into which his mistaken belief led him. If he has to act in the agony of the moment, he will equally be exonerated for any reasonable mistake,

5.3 Conditions of Valid Consent

It is a principle of Common Law that if true consent to a treatment is given by a competent person, the treatment is lawful. But for this to hold true, the consent must be given to a competent person; it must be informed; and it must be free. If any of these requirements are lacking, the consent will be treated as invalid and any treatment carried out under it will be held to be unlawful.

5.4 Competence

Whether a person is competent to give a true consent is a question of fact. It is — in legal jargon — a "jury issue", and the doctor or nurse seeking a consent will have to act as his own jury: he will have to judge whether the patient understands his position and can make a rational judgement about whether to agree to have the proposed treatment or not. Not an easy question in many cases, and often requiring a fine judgement based on close questioning. If a dispute arises, the court has to proceed by the same method.

5.5 Informed Consent

The principle that even if a patient has ostensibly given his consent, it may be vitiated by non-disclosure of relevant information, has been recognised in various common law jurisdictions. Theoretically, if a patient has to be fully apprised of relevant information before consenting to treatment, he ought to be given a wide range of information. He ought to be told the gravity of his condition and its likely developments; the nature of the proposed treatment, and all the risks attendant upon it; and the possible alternative treatments and their likely outcome.

A court would probably resolve the question of the extent of the necessary disclosure by examining the purpose for which the information was required — that is, the making of a responsible decision. It would then assess the precise circumstances and the relevance of the information which would have been disclosed for that purpose. If it found that something which any patient ought for this purpose to have been told had been unjustifiably omitted, it would hold that any consent given was vitiated.

But this merely conceals the problems, and does not solve them. It is, for example, recognised medically to be desirable not to divulge certain risks to a patient who may not have the emotional or intellectual capacity to accept the information without excessive distortion of his judgement or worsening of his condition. In such a case, a conflict of duty arises for the doctor, in which the duty to care prevails over the duty to give all the relevant information. He might abrogate his responsibility for the real interests of his patient if he told him everything.

Again, a doctor may well not know all the contingencies or chances as to how matters may turn out. He may innocently be mistaken as to some important fact; or he may be mistaken in holding a particular medical opinion, and so may some or even all of his colleagues. Is he to be at risk if his lack of knowledge or mistake is the unwitting cause of unforeseen disaster for the patient?

There is little in existing legal decisions to help either doctor or patient in such involved situations. The balanced assessment of all the relevant factors has been accepted, in a number of Common Law court decisions, as the correct approach. So, in deciding whether he ought to disclose something to his patient which, in the interests of his patient, he would not normally disclose, the doctor has the unenviable job of assessing how great the risk is that the patient's consent will be given on inadequate grounds, as against the extent of the risk that, if the disclosure is made, the patient's condition will be affected by the knowledge, or his judgement materially impaired.

In assessing whether or not a risk should be disclosed to a patient, the doctor would no doubt bear in mind that while a small risk of a small side-effect would count for little, a small risk of a very serious result would weigh heavily. Indeed, it might well prevail in law, unless the doctor could show that the risk of an even more serious deterioration in the patient's condition would have resulted from disclosure.

In assessing the right balance, a question would arise in law as to whether the true test is:

(a) Would a reasonable *doctor* practising in the relevant field have disclosed the risk? (This entails consideration of the current standards and practices in the appropriate medical field); or
(b) Is the risk something which a reasonable man in the position of the *patient* would regard as significant in making his decision as to whether to undergo the treatment proposed (whatever the doctors may think)?

Conflicting decisions as to this choice have been made in different jurisdictions. In England and Wales it is likely that the former approach would be adopted, on the grounds that one is seeking to do justice between the competing claims of doctor and patient and that if there is a residual risk, it should fall on the person whose natural misfortune has given rise to the possibility of such a risk.

It is likely that if a patient asks specifically about the risks or about a specific risk carried by a proposed treatment, the doctor would be bound in law to tell him all he knows, unless in an unusual case there were some overwhelming reason which might justify prevarication. Equally if a doctor realises that his knowledge of the risks is limited, he would be bound to inform the patient accordingly, with the same exception for some overwhelming reason to the contrary.

Special problems arise when the treatment envisaged is not fully established, or is irreversible, or if the limits of its efficacy are not known. Disclosure of the limits of knowledge would in general be required, but difficulties about the extent of the information which should be disclosed would certainly arise, and could only be resolved by judgement in the particular circumstances.

5.6 Free Consent

The law asserts the principle of free consent, but in a negative rather than a positive way: it rules out any consent obtained by duress or fraud. It is axiomatic that if a practitioner obtained by coercive or deceptive acts or words a consent in respect of any treatment, the consent would be vitiated. This would be so even if the consent is given in writing, but the coercion or deception is by word of mouth.

But it is difficult to find any principle of law which would invalidate a consent given by a person, capable of making a rational judgement, where he is subject to inducements or fears about his position or treatment which are not brought about by the doctor. This is the classic situation in which one or other of the new techniques might be used on a prisoner or patient who, while otherwise able to exercise a rational judgement, may be subject to such "hidden" restraints or inducements. He may (perhaps quite wrongly) think that if he consents to the treatment, he will obtain a benefit (an earlier release, for example, if he is in a Special Hospital), or that if he does not consent he will suffer some disadvantage.

In general, the Common Law treats competent adults as free to decide for themselves, when their decision is not improperly influenced by others. Thus one finds, in a parallel situation, that an accused person's confession will be held to be vitiated, and therefore inadmissible, if it was induced by some fear excited, or hope held out, by a person in authority; but that it will be held to be admissible if such fears or hopes as the accused had were not created or increased by anyone in authority.

There seems to be no existing rule of law which would vitiate a consent to treatment given by any prisoner or detained patient merely because he was detained and therefore subject to certain constraints, or merely because when giving his consent he was actually subject to fears or hopes about his present or future position which were not induced in him by anyone in the prison or hospital.

5.7 Mental Health Act

We have already seen (in Chapter 3) that certain sections of the Mental Health Act 1959 authorise the compulsory admission of mental health patients. It is not certain whether in every case this means that, after such admission, clinical treatment can be given compulsorily, i.e. without consent. That question has not been decided by the courts, but it has been decided that medical and nursing staff have the protection of Section 141 of the Act if they exercise physical control over a detained patient without his consent. This means that even if their power to apply physical restraint to such patients without consent is in any way limited, they have statutory protection if they have acted in good faith and with reasonable care. There is some support for the view that the same would be true in respect of clinical treatment, in addition to acts of physical control. But on the issue whether under the Act they have power at all to give treatment to such patients without consent, the better view is that they do have such power. There has been considerable legal argument about this question, but if this view is correct, it follows that, for detained mental health patients, this is another exception to the basic rule that without consent treatment will be a civil wrong.

5.8 The Butler Committee

The difficulty of predicting what degree of necessity would justify medical action is formidable, and in 1975 a Committee under the Chairmanship of Lord Butler made recommendations in order to clarify the situation at least so far as mentally abnormal offenders are concerned. It said that:

(a) If a patient is able to appreciate what is involved but refuses to give his consent, a treatment could be given if

(i) it is the minimum interference with the patient necessary to prevent him from behaving violently or otherwise being a danger to himself or others. But the treatment must not be hazardous or irreversible.

or (ii) it is necessary to save the patient's life. In this instance, it is suggested that the treatment should not be hazardous or irreversible. In other words, if the patient's life is at stake, it is better to use even a hazardous or irreversible treatment, if this is the only possible course.

or (iii) it is necessary to prevent the patient from deteriorating. In this instance the treatment must not be irreversible.

(b) If the patient cannot appreciate what is involved, any treatment thought necessary by the doctor (within the limits of professional ethics) can be given, save that if it is an irreversible treatment, a second independent psychiatric opinion should be obtained (unless, in turn, delay in obtaining that opinion would cause or increase a danger to life).

5.9 Butler and the Law

It is interesting to see what would be the effect of these recommendations on the legal position. For the unconscious (or otherwise incapable) patient, the Butler recommendation does not mention, though it may well imply, the balancing process which the law would require as a condition of justification for the doctor's action in treating without consent. For the conscious resisting patient, whose life is not at risk, the prohibition against any hazardous or irreversible treatment to prevent violence or danger to the patient or others in an emergency shuts a door which the existing law would leave open. There are obviously powerful reasons why even such a treatment should be used in appropriate circumstances, though such circumstances must be very rare. If the lives of 100 people in a hospital or prison depended on a doctor treating one patient (without his consent) and in the emergency no other means of averting the danger save a hazardous or irreversible treatment were available to the doctor, he would (in law) not only be entitled to balance all the factors and decide to apply the treatment, but might possibly be under a duty to the others to apply it. A blanket prohibition makes sense in the context of a situation where choices of treatment are available, but in that context does little but state the obvious. In a situation where there is no choice of different treatments, a prohibition might well cause considerable agony of mind to a doctor who had to weigh the lives of others against the effect of treatment on the patient. Both hazard and irreversibility are involved in the techniques which we have to consider, and some of them are not fully established.

5.10 Butler and Reality

Another feature of the Butler recommendations is that they deal with supposed facts, not opinions ("is able to appreciate", "is not of a hazardous or irreversible nature", "is necessary"). This approach is fine for rule-making; it is not so fine for practical situations where facts are not clear-cut. Again the law may do better in that, so far as one can predict, it is likely that a court would take into account the fact that a doctor had reached a reasonable, albeit mistaken, view in deciding what the factors were and how to act.

5.11 The White Paper 'Review of the Mental Health Act'

The difficulties and dangers which flow from the ambiguity with which facts present themselves in practical situations were taken up in the White Paper in 1978. It proposed broadly to endorse the Butler recommendations but, as a protection for both the patient and the doctor, to extend the requirements for a second opinion considerably, even to a point where they could become unwieldy and bureaucratic.

In the event, the Butler Committee's proposals have still not been implemented.

So far, we have attempted to examine the ethical and legal safeguards which at present exist, or are proposed, to protect people in this country against the possible misuse of new techniques such as those described in Chapter 2. But are they enough? Or do we need other safeguards?

6
The Problem Re-examined

6.1 The Background

The question whether any of the techniques under discussion in this Report should cause special concern, and whether they should therefore be regulated in some special way, has to be viewed in the general context of the many ways in which people seek to influence the attitudes and behaviour of others.

Sometimes they do it with the deliberate intention of influencing their fellows. But many human acts, and many events brought about by the forces of nature, have the unintended consequence of causing substantial changes in personality and behaviour. Bereavement, illness, suffering a criminal assault, and natural or economic disasters — as well as a major win on the pools — are examples of such events. The web of cause and effect is far-flung.

Social institutions, too, employ powerful coercive mechanisms to produce desired patterns in the behaviour of society's members. A society's corpus of law is one of its most potent and pervasive tools. Imprisonment, as a means of enforcing the criminal law, is another, though surprisingly little is known of its actual effects in changing behaviour. In our culture the education of children is compulsory, and can be far-ranging in its effects.

Apart from techniques adopted by society as a whole, our culture permits many other practices designed to "push" human beings into desired forms of behaviour: commercial advertising, political campaigning and religious evangelisation are only some of many examples. So one can see that the mere alteration of attitudes or behaviour, whether deliberate or unintended, is not by itself a bogey of which we need be frightened. If there is a bogey, it lies elsewhere.

The new techniques which we have described therefore raise two questions. Do they differ in some important respects from other forms of pressure which our society already employs? If so, should society seek to regulate their application in some special way?

6.2 The Citadel of Personality

One of the concepts on which our culture places a specially high value is that of personal autonomy, which includes the freedom to determine, within the limits set by nature and nurture, what kind of a person one wishes to be. While the claims of others necessarily constrain what we are free to *do*, they do not constrain to the same extent what we are free to *be* — our thoughts, beliefs, opinions, feelings, tastes and attitudes. We may, or may not, be content with our present personalities, but we wish to remain free to determine for ourselves whether to try and change them, and how. If the available means for change are understandable, predictable and avoidable, we must choose whether to use them or not. But the decision becomes more difficult if those means involve a complex technique beyond the understanding of the ordinary layman, especially if it operates by manipulating his personality in ways which he cannot see happening, and which he cannot prevent once the treatment is applied.

We believe that these are the leading features of the new treatments which raise the problems to which this Report is addressed. Rightly or wrongly, they may be regarded as an insidious subversion of the citadel of the human personality. In that respect at least, they differ from techniques with which we have long been familiar, and they may therefore raise new problems.

6.3 Regulation by Society

At least since the time of John Stuart Mill, it has been accepted as a basic principle of a liberal society that people who have reached an age of discretion should be free to choose what they will or will not do, providing they are willing to live with the consequences of their choices, and that they cause no demonstrable harm to the interests of others in the process. In this country, we have been apt in recent years to prune from our law some of its "illiberal" features which seemed to offend against that principle, such as the prohibition of homosexual conduct between consenting adults.

So long as that principle continues to command general assent, we see no reason why society should prohibit or regulate any new treatments or techniques, even if they do subvert the citadel of personality, *where they are administered between consenting adults* — that is, where somebody deliberately chooses such treatment with a full knowledge and understanding of what he is letting himself in for, and has it administered to him by a competent practitioner whose only concern is the benefit of the patient.

Where such a bargain is freely struck, we see no case for overriding it. On the contrary, its prohibition would deprive people of the opportunity of receiving treatment which they (and only they have the right to decide) see as being for their benefit, and would in addition restrict advances in medicine. There is one exception to this: we consider that society would be justified in prohibiting a form of treatment which resulted in a grave or total and irreversible loss of the patient's own autonomy.

In what one might call this "private area", therefore, society's concern should be limited to ensuring that, where such techniques are being administered, the "consenting adults" principle is observed — and that, in support of it, the public is protected from incompetent or unscrupulous practitioners.

Where the proposed treatment involves physical intervention, as in the case of psychosurgery or ECT, which would constitute battery if it were compulsorily administered, the present law largely gives that protection; likewise, the drugs which we have described are only available on prescription. In all these cases, there is the additional protection of established medical ethics.

But where there is no physical intervention, as in the cases of behaviour therapy and psychotherapy, the position is less satisfactory. Here, as we have explained in Chapter 5, there is no battery in law, for the law of battery protects only the body, and not the mind. As it now stands, the patient's only remedy would be a civil action for negligence, in which he would have to prove that he had suffered damage as the foreseeable result of a therapist's failure to use "due skill and care". That can often be a very difficult task for a plaintiff to discharge. Moreover, in the case of these treatments, as we have explained in Chapter 4, there is no code of professional ethics which effectively binds "lay" practitioners. Here, therefore, there is a case for rather more regulation that presently exists.

6.4 Imposition by Society

If that were all there was to it, our Report could end here. But matters are more complex than that. If society is to protect the freedom of its members, it must protect them — through its "law and order" role — from individuals who might do them harm. Society also claims the role of a benevolent parent, and seeks to alleviate the misfortunes of its members who, through no fault of their own, lack the competence to take care of themselves — or who seek to do themselves irreparable harm, as in the case of the heroin addict. In either of these roles, society might feel justified in causing techniques of behaviour modification to be applied to some of its members over whom it exercises power by holding them "captive" — that is, convicted prisoners, mental patients in detention, and children in care.

Then, the question is not whether society has any business to *prevent* bargains from being struck between its members in the "private sector", but whether it has any right to use its collective power in the public sector to *cause* the citadels of some of its members' personalities to be subverted in the absence of any such bargains.

Most people's instinctive responses to that question would probably be a resounding "No". It seems at first sight outrageous that society, or any of its agencies, should have power to force people to undergo treatments which will change their personalities in ways they cannot control and do not want.

Yet there are difficulties with that answer. Some mental patients are already being compulsorily treated in hospital, to their great benefit. But more important, society by common consent already uses ways of influencing or controlling the behaviour of its members in several spheres, regardless of their wishes. Imprisonment is one example; some would say compulsory education is another. Both can have profound and irreversible effects, yet neither prisoners nor schoolchildren are given any choice in the matter.

If we already have such laws and practices, what is there to prevent a future Government persuading Parliament to authorise the compulsory subversion of certain personalities if some public authority judges it expedient for their own good, or for the good of others? After all, the United Kingdon (almost uniquely amongst the world's nations) has no written constitution containing a catalogue of entrenched rights on which the State may not trespass.

That being so, what is there to prevent the new techniques from being used to mitigate or remove the danger of violent criminals and the nuisance of social deviants and misfits, and so to save the rest of the community a great deal of suffering, damage, trouble and expense?

6.5 The Prevailing Social Ethic

How one answers that question depends, ultimately, on whether one believes that there are areas of forbidden ground on which the organised powers of the State must never be allowed to trespass, and how one draws the boundaries of such areas.

If there are none — if, given sufficiently potent arguments, there are no limits to what the State may be allowed to do to its subjects in the interests of what it judges to be the common good — then it must also be allowed to perform personality changes on its recalcitrant subjects if the case for doing so is sufficiently strong. And if, one day, that were to become the general consensus of the population as expressed by its elected representatives, there is nothing in our constitutional arrangements which could prevent that consensus from being enacted into law. Anyone who disagreed would then only be left with the final option of emigration — if the law had not by then also closed that escape route.

But that is certainly not the prevailing ethic of our present society.

Quite the contrary. A great deal of misgiving has arisen precisely because many people fear that, by slow degrees, the techniques we have described may become so refined that it will be increasingly difficult to resist the temptation to use them in the supposed interests of the community, rather than only in the interests of the individual to whom they might be administered — not to mention the further justification that what is being done *is* in the interests of the individual, even if he cannot see that for himself.

There *is* in fact an area of forbidden ground. But what are its boundaries? How can the current misgivings be reconciled with the general acceptance of compulsory techniques for the containment of prisoners, the treatment of mental patients who are not competent to give their consent, and the compulsory education of children?

Society appears to judge that question according to principles somewhat like these:-

1) in the general case, compulsory procedures which have the effect of modifying people's behaviour are justified where they are imposed openly for the manifest benefit of every member of the group concerned — as in the case of compulsory education;
2) in individual cases, such procedures are justified if they are imposed for the manifest benefit of the individual concerned, on the authority of someone who has no other interest than the promotion of that benefit, and is answerable for what he does both to the law and to an ethical tribunal of his professional peers — as in the case of the mental patient who is not competent to give or refuse his consent;
3) they are not justified in any other case — apart perhaps from extreme emergencies such as an imminent danger to life or limb.

Imprisonment might, at first sight, seem to be an anomalous case to which these principles do not apply. If it is, the anomaly is explicable on a number of grounds. No one need suffer imprisonment unless he chooses: all he need do is to obey the law. Society incarcerates him to protect itself, to deter others, and to express its revulsion for his crime and its desire for his punishment. The "reform of the prisoner" — that is a modification of his future behaviour — is only one of the purposes of his imprisonment (except perhaps in the case of the currently fashionable "short sharp shock" sentence). And this is not imposed by the State as such, but by independent members of its judiciary who are charged with weighing all the factors in public, and are publicly accountable for their decisions. It is not the aim of imprisonment to perform an insidious subversion of the citadel of personality: if conditions in our prisons were as they ought to be, the long-term effect of a prison sentence would, at least on the face of it, be both resistible and reversible.

Compulsory education too, displays some special features. It is primarily designed to make knowledge accessible to those who do not already have it. The means employed are open and visible: they do not involve any arcane technology, nor were they designed for the alleviation or cure of medically recognised disorders — indeed, there would be a public outcry if the State attempted to use such methods for insidiously indoctrinating the young. And for that very reason, in the United Kingdom importance is attached to the decentralised structure of the education system: while central government may ultimately foot the bill, it is the individual schools and the Local Education Authorities which decide the content and method of what is taught.

6.6 Guiding Principles

If we accept these principles, it would follow that compulsory treatment to modify behaviour would be allowed, but only if,

1) there is an imminent danger to someone's life or limb, which can only be averted by these means; *or*
2) a) the subject is not competent to give or refuse his consent; *and*
   b) the treatment is manifestly for the subject's benefit, in the judgement of someone who has no interest other than the promotion of that benefit; *and*
   c) that person is answerable for his decisions both to the law and to an ethical tribunal of his professional peers.

Accordingly, no such treatment should ever be administered, otherwise than in an extreme emergency,

1) to anyone who, being competent to do so, refuses his consent; *or*
2) by anyone who serves any interests which conflict with those of the subject; *or*
3) by anyone who is not answerable for his decisions both to the law and to his professional peers.

On the assumption that these propositions would command a wide measure of support, we shall try in the next Chapter to devise some rules for the situations with which we are here concerned, and to propose some safeguards designed to make it more likely that those rules will be observed in practice.

7
Some General Proposals

7.1 The Ideal Rules

We draw a clear distinction between two situations:-

1) Where a medical (or other) practitioner, treating a person as his patient, seeks to cure or alleviate some medically recognised disorder *diagnosed* in that patient, by the application of some procedure designed for that purpose;
2) Where someone (whether or not a professional practitioner), with the object of modifying or controlling someone else's attitudes or behaviour, applies a procedure designed to cure or alleviate a medically recognised disorder to a person who has *not been diagnosed* as suffering from any such disorder.

We are concerned with both these situations, but the distinction is important, and is not always made clear enough.

We are satisfied that the second of these situations is one in which no professional practitioner should ever play any part — whether in applying the procedure, advising it or condoning it.

But what of the first? What must a doctor do when faced with a patient who displays patterns of behaviour of which his society disapproves? Here the position is no different from that which obtains when any patient is presented to any practitioner: the doctor must first decide whether the patient is suffering from any recognised disorder. (As the 1980 Reith Lectures have shown, that question itself can be controversial). Next he must consider what treatments are available, weighing the pros and cons and the competence or otherwise of his patients, as we have set out in Chapter 5. And, finally, he must decide what to do exclusively in the patient's interest, *not* to satisfy others in his immediate circle who may dislike his conduct, find him difficult to manage, or even regard him (rightly or wrongly) as a danger. None of these reasons justifies treating a patient who refuses to be treated.

These rules are easy to state, but a good deal less easy to apply. And there are countries in the world in which some practitioners are willing to certify patients as medically disordered if all that is found to be wrong with them is a perfectly rational disagreement with the way in which their country is governed, combined with an insistence on making their views known to others. One might at least have hoped that internationally agreed catalogues or glossaries of diseases would not offer such practitioners even apparent support. But that does not seem to be the case; the current International Classification of Diseases of the World Health Organisation, for example, contains the following remarkable entry under "Mental Disorders":-

312.0 Unsocialised disturbance of conduct: Disorders characterised by behaviour such as defiance, disobedience, quarrelsomeness, aggression, destructive behaviour, tantrums, solitary stealing, lying, teasing, bullying and disturbed relationships with others. The defiance may sometimes take the form of sexual misconduct.

Such a personality disorder is fortunately not a certifiable mental illness in the United Kingdom. At least the first part of that description might have characterised any band of determined reformers, including the Twelve Apostles.

However, assuming that a practitioner has the professional integrity to resist such temptations of diagnosis, and has a patient who understands and can freely consent to his treatment, it may not be all plain sailing. Matters will often fall short of the ideal for the reasons set out in Chapter 5 — the risks and uncertainties of treatment, and the doubts about the patient's understanding and competence, will often make for hesitation and difficulty. Nowhere will these shortfalls occur more frequently that in the field with which this Report deals.

We therefore propose one more general rule and a set of safeguards designed to promote its application in practice.

7.2 Making Shortfalls Good

The rule is simple: wherever there is a shortfall from the ideal state of affairs, it should if at all possible be made good before the treatment is carried out. So, for example,

a) whenever any treatment entails known and important adverse effects, or known risks of such effects, or is subject to important uncertainties, all these should be fully explained to the patient to the limit of his understanding;
b) whenever there are important constraints on the patient's competence or freedom to give consent, those constraints should be removed before the consent is given.

But if — as will often be the case — the ideal state of affairs (or something sufficiently close to it) cannot be achieved by such means, then the shortfall must be made good in some other way.

7.3 Second Opinions

A well-established method of remedying such defects, when practitioners themselves are in doubt about the rightness of a contemplated course of treatment, is the obtaining of a second professional opinion. This has often proved valuable either in confirming the doubt, or in dispelling it. We hope that it will continue to be used whenever the practitioner in charge has any real doubt about one of the professional aspects of his diagnosis, or of the preferred treatment he has it in mind to administer.

But there are important limitations to this safeguard. A second professional opinion is only competent to express an expert view on professional matters, and not on any others. It may make a valuable contribution on matters of diagnosis, or on questions such as the risks of adverse effects, the extent of uncertainty, or the prospects of success of a treatment. But a practitioner is no better (and sometimes perhaps less) qualified than anyone else to give opinions outside the field of his expertise, and some of the possible shortfalls from the ideal state cannot be made good by any professional expertise.

For example, though a psychiatrist or psychologist may be able to cast some useful light on the degree of understanding of a patient about matters which concern him, the question of the sufficiency of that understanding is not a professional one, but rather one for which lay evaluation may be more suitable. Again, a lawyer may be better qualified than a doctor to judge whether a consent given by a prisoner or a mental patient is sufficiently free.

There are, in short, some defects which can be better remedied by obtaining a lay second opinion rather than a professional one — using the word "lay" here merely in the sense of not coming from colleagues of the same discipline. Such an opinion should not attempt to cover matters of exclusively professional competence, on which it would have no value. But we believe that in many cases it could usefully complement the professional opinion of doctors, psychologists and others — and in some it could be essential in putting forward a view which falls outside the professional competence of any of these practitioners.

We believe that such lay second opinions should be obtained whenever there is an important defect in the patient's understanding, or in his competence or freedom to give consent. What is needed in such cases is an opinion from someone who can represent that patient's interests, but who is not subject to his disabilities. The remaining questions then are who that should be, and how one can best ensure that his opinion is sought, and that it is given its proper weight.

7.4 A Patient's Advocate

A patient's advocate will need several qualifications: he must know or be able to learn enough about the patient and his circumstances to be able to put himself into the patient's position, and to judge what is in his best interests; he must be able to understand the professional aspects if they are properly explained to him; and he must be wholly independent of any authorities who may have an interest of their own in having the treatment administered.

Some patients will have a suitable relative or friend who can act in this capacity. Failing that, there may be a suitable probation or welfare officer. But if none of these can be found, we suggest that there should be some panel from which a suitable patient's advocate can be drawn — rather like the duty solicitor scheme in our Magistrates' Courts to provide legal advice and representation for defendants who cannot find their own, or the panel of lay members and lawyers on whom the Mental Health Review Tribunals can call. The recently-formed Advocacy Alliance might also extend its activities into this field.

7.5 Options for Enforcement

The next question is how one ensures that the rules and safeguards are in fact applied and used in all the cases where they are needed. Here, there are two options: the compulsory and the voluntary.

In a compulsory system, the law or an administrative regulation would lay it down that, in circumstances there exhaustively defined, treatments of the kind which would also be defined could not be given unless someone (again defined in the regulation) had first certified that it could be. This has the merit of some degree of certainty, but it also has several demerits.

The first is that such a system is necessarily formal, cumbersome and bureaucratic. It could not be brought into effect without a good deal of form-filling, and the creation of new institutions and their accompanying administrations. But there is a second, and more subtle, demerit: such a system entails the possibility of an effective veto over a clinician's freedom to treat his patient as he thinks best. That runs counter to all the instincts and traditions of the medical profession.

As an alternative, therefore, we would suggest a more informal, and essentially voluntary, system. Under that, a clinician would still be free to decide, as he does now, whether to administer any particular treatment to any particular patient. But whenever he is in doubt about that patient's ability to understand what this will or may involve for him, or his competence or freedom to give or refuse consent to it, he should seek a suitable lay advocate for that patient who is truly independent, has no concern other than the patient's own interest, and is free of any of the patient's own disabilities. Having obtained that advocate's opinion, the clinician should then give it its proper weight before deciding whether or not to administer the treatment.

That has the merit of not interfering with clinical freedom. But it has the obvious demerit that, without more, it would supply no incentives for any clinician either to obtain such an opinion, or to give it any weight.

In order to provide those incentives, we propose that the safeguard which we have suggested should be made the norm of professional conduct, both as a matter of law and as a matter of professional ethics. In that way, a clinician would still be free not to follow it, but if his conduct were later called into question, he would risk being disciplined by his professional bodies, and ordered to pay damages in a court of law, unless he could justify his conduct — and the burden of justification would be on him.

By way of illustration let us suppose that a patient has homicidal and suicidal tendencies and is severely depressed. He has not responded to antidepressant medication and his doctor is convinced that he will benefit from ECT. The doctor may be reinforced in that view by a second professional opinion from a colleague. He offers the treatment to the patient who refuses on grounds which appear to be delusional, e.g. "I am born to suffer, no one must help me." Should the doctor simply accept the refusal, or should he override it? We think that before he does either he should call in a lay advocate, perhaps a close relative who knows the patient well, or the patient's social worker, or even, in some circumstances, the patient's solicitor. They are told the medical facts about the disorder, the type of treatment being offered, its hazards, its advantages, the hazards of not giving it. They are then asked to advise the doctor what in their lay opinions they think he ought to do.

We believe that such a procedure would provide sufficient incentives for the protection of patients. Where any substantial doubt existed, the clinician would have every interest in applying our suggested safeguards, for he could only afford to ignore it at the risk of subsequent disciplinary action, and of judgement being awarded against him in court. Moreover, he would ensure that what he had done — diagnosis, consultations, opinions expressed and treatment given — was all properly recorded in case he needed to rely on it later if his conduct was called into question. Strange though it may seem, there is at present no obligation to record any of this.

This solution also has the merit of probably not needing legislation. If the General Medical Council, the British Medical Association, and all other competent professional bodies were to require the use of our suggested safeguard as a matter of professional ethics, there is every likelihood that the courts would follow suit. Only if they did not, would legislation be required.

To all this there is one exception, and that is the emergency which comes about so quickly that there is no time for applying any safeguards at all. In our view, if the emergency presents a clear and present danger of loss of life or serious physical injury, to the patient or anyone else, the clinician must continue to be entitled to administer the least hazardous known treatment, if that is the only way to avert the danger. But we would not be inclined to make that exception any wider.

7.6 General and Specific

It will be seen that, in this Chapter, we draw no distinction between the different kinds of treatment for the modification of behaviour or attitudes which we have considered earlier in this Report. That is deliberate, for we believe that the same principles apply to them all. The application of these principles depends not on the nature of the treatment, but on its effects (beneficial and adverse), its known hazards, and the uncertainties to which it is at any time subject. All these may change in the course of time, as the treatments and the professional knowledge about them are refined.

Nor do we draw any distinction between medical practitioners and those whose professional skills stem from other disciplines. That is because we believe that, in the questions which we are here considering, no such distinction can validly be drawn. Whenever anyone has at his command special skills which can place him in a position of power or influence over others who are under some important disability, because he is specially placed to manipulate them (whether by the use of those skills or by his professional alignment with the apparatus of social authority), he owes those others a paramount obligation to use his special position only in their interests, and not in his own or that of his employers. And that proposition holds good for everyone who has been trained in the exercise of any such professional skills — for the clinical psychologist and the psychotherapists no less than for the surgeon or physician.

Nor, finally, have we distinguished between different categories of patients under disabilities, such as children in care, prisoners, persons on probation, and compulsory or voluntary patients in mental hospitals, special or general. That too is deliberate, for what matters in every case is the patient's ability to understand what any treatment entails for him, and to give his free consent. Our principles apply whenever any patient suffers an important impairment, whatever may be its proximate cause. And our suggested safeguards should be used whenever that is the case, in order to seek to remedy the defect in understanding or consent, and so approximate more closely to the ideal state of affairs.

For ease of reference we have produced a flow-chart to illustrate how our suggested rules and safeguards would be applied, and this is reproduced at the end of this Report.

7.7 Treatment for Mentally Ill Prisoners

There remains one other problem, which is in some respects the obverse of the one we have been considering all this time. It is the problem of prisoners who are mentally ill, who need treatment for their disorder, but who cannot obtain it because they are in prison.

In theory, such prisoners can be transferred to psychiatric hospitals (see Chapter 3). But there is now such difficulty in finding hospital places for them that some mentally ill prisoners have to remain within prison hospitals. Occasionally they require compulsory treatment for their illness, which can only be given to patients detained in mental hospitals under the appropriate certificate, and safeguards. It seems indefensible that prisoners should be deprived of necessary treatment which is available to all other citizens, merely because they are offenders.

We therefore recommend that a small number of well-equipped prison hospitals should be designated as mental hospitals, so that prisoners could be detained there under a Mental Health Act Certificate. We propose that such a certificate should be given by two psychiatrists outside the Prison Medical Service and should be subject to the same appeal procedures as other certificates made under the Act. Such a new arrangement should be used only for prisoners suffering either from mental illness or severe subnormality. Current psychiatric practice in the UK confines the term "mental illness" to psychotic, severe neurotic, and organic conditions, and excludes personality disorders and subnormality. This arrangement would therefore, rightly, exclude people suffering from (non-severe) subnormality or from psychopathic disorder.

Three main problems would arise from this proposal. First, the extension of Mental Health Act appeal procedures into the prison system would create some administrative problems for both the Home Office and the Mental Health Review Tribunals, but we do not believe these to be insurmountable.

Secondly, there may be an occasional case where a prisoner still requires compulsory hospital treatment when his earliest date of release from prison arrives. In ideal circumstances he should then be transferred to an ordinary hospital, but our proposal is prompted largely by the fact that ideal circumstances do not prevail; there is no guarantee that transfer will take place, as hospitals have the right to refuse such patients. In these circumstances, we believe that the prisoner should remain in the designated prison hospital until the date when his prison sentence has finally expired; during that time the Home Office should negotiate with the DHSS to find him a suitable placement after his sentence expires. In the unhappy eventuality of no such placement being found, he should be discharged.

The third problem is that the compulsory treatment of mentally sick people within the prison system could be seen as an infringement of their civil rights. While it is certainly a less satisfactory arrangement than treatment within an ordinary mental hospital, we regard the present situation, in which some very sick patients receive no treatment at all, as an even greater loss of a civil right, namely the right to proper medical care, compulsory if need be, for a recognisable mental illness.

8
Our Conclusions

The consequences of our proposals may not all be immediately obvious, and we shall therefore spell them out here.

1. *No* professional practitioner — whether medical, paramedical (e.g. nurses) or non-medical — should ever use his special skills to administer recondite techniques designed to modify attitudes or behaviour which those skills specially enable him to practise, for any purpose other than to cure or alleviate some known and recognised medical disorder in his patient or client. It follows that non-medical practitioners should be subjected in this respect to the same ethical rules as medical ones, with the same adverse consequences to them if they infringe those rules — and with the same collective support from their professions if they obey them.

2. The principles and rules we have outlined should govern *all* the techniques which we have considered, and any others which may be discovered or developed in the future. We do not therefore recommend that any particular technique — such as psychosurgery — should be absolutely banned, nor that any of them should be granted any form of exemption from the rules. The more unpredictable the results and the more likely any irreversible side-effects, the more important will it be to obtain the best-informed and most freely given consent from the patient, and to use the most stringent safeguards to substitute for that consent if it cannot be obtained — for example if, because the patient is held captive in an institution, his consent may be constrained. Even where the benefit to the patient is highly likely, and the risks of any harm are slight, his consent should only be dispensed with if he is manifestly incompetent to give it; if he *is* competent to give it, his positive refusal should only be overriden where there is a clear and present danger to life or limb. In all these cases except the last, any shortfall in the necessary consent must be made up by consent obtained from someone else who is independent and competent to give it, as a lay advocate, on the patient's behalf, and a proper record must be kept of the procedure that is followed.

3. We offer no comfort for the hard-pressed administrators of our penal,

mental and other institutions. We sympathise with their wish to procure the benefits of modern science for the reduction of disorder and disruption within those institutions. But we believe that even the slightest concession which would make it possible in some cases to substitute their consent for that of an inmate, or their administrative considerations for the clinical judgements of independent health professionals, could offer dangerous temptations to future generations of their successors.

4. The clearest possible line of separation should be drawn, and maintained, between what is thought by an independent clinician to be in the best interests of his patient, and what is thought by administrators to be in the best interests of their institutions. The clinician's task is to develop and use the best techniques for curing or alleviating his patients' disorders; the administrators' task is to develop and use the best techniques for maintaining order within their institutions. These tasks are wholly distinct, and should never be confused. In the long run, the greatest risk is that one day, for what may appear the best of motives, they will be.

5. It is precisely because the inmates of institutions are branded as either "mad" or "bad" by the general public, and because any consent given by such an inmate will always be suspect since its freedom must be in question, that we believe that specially stringent safeguards need to be erected before any sophisticated techniques of behaviour modification can be administered to him.

6. The best long-term guarantee of such safeguards lies in confiding them to independent members of independent health professions, neither individually nor collectively subject to direction (or, as far as possible, even influence) by potentially authoritarian state institutions, and reinforced by codes of professional ethics, and ultimately by the law.

7. To ensure that such a system of safeguards will continue to function effectively, it should operate as openly as possible, subject to the scrutiny of the press, and so of the general public.

8. No system of safeguards in any field can guarantee that any society, even the most civilised and politically mature, will not one day degenerate into intolerance, totalitarianism and oppression if the stresses upon it become too great. That has been demonstrated, tragically, in the 1930s and more recently. But safeguards of the kind we propose can at least make such tragedies less likely, or delay their consummation — provided their maintenance is not entrusted to any governmental institutions. That is the principal reason why we have not made any proposals for the official licensing and control either of the techniques with which we are concerned, or of the institutions in which they can be administered, but have preferred to distribute the responsibility for applying the necessary safeguards widely among the members of independent professions.

9. In the result, if any future administration wished to use sophistic-

ated techniques of this kind, not for the cure or alleviation of disorders but for social control, within institutions or outside them, it would need first to recruit and train officials willing to administer them without the constraints imposed by the ethical and legal restrictions applied to members of the health professions. Given a sufficiently determined government, and a sufficiently subservient Parliament, press and public, that could doubtless be done. But at least it could hardly be done in secret, and it would not entail the prior corruption of the health professions.

Bibliography

BIBLIOGRAPHY

1 George J. Annas: "Psychosurgery; procedural safeguards", *Hastings Center Report*, April 1977, pp.11-13.

2 Aileen Ballantyne: "Common questions on children in mental hospitals", *The Guardian*, 17 November, 1980.

3. B. M. Barraclough and N. A. Mitchell-Heggs: "Use of neurosurgery for psychological disorder in British Isles during 1974-6", *BMJ*, 9 December 1978, pp.1591-1593.

4. D. E. Blackman: "Ethical standards for behaviour modification", *British Journal of Criminology*, October 1979, pp. 420-448.

5. Paul Bowden: "Medical practice: defendants and prisoners", *Journal of Medical Ethics*, 1976, vol. 2, pp. 163-172.

6. Edgar M. Brenner: "Behaviour modification", reprinted from *Criminal Defense Techniques*, Matthew Bender & Co. Ltd., New York, 1976.

7. British Medical Journal: "Mentally disordered offenders", *BMJ*, Leader, No. 6155, 6 January, 1979, pp. 1-2.

8. Citizens Commission on Human Rights (sponsored by the Church of Scientology): *Drugs in Prisons*, compilation of articles includes reprints of:
(i) Dr. C. H. McCleary: "Treatment of psychopaths with Depixol", *Prison Medical Journal* No. 18;
(ii) O. W. S. Fitzgerald, "Chemical treatment of sexual offenders", *PMJ*, No. 18, Summer 1978, pp. 25-29;
(iii) Editorial in *PMJ*, No. 19 by Dr. Mary Ellis;
(iv) "Drug treatment in prisons" in *PROP*, paper of the national prisoners' movement, Vol. 2, No. 2, April-May 1977.

9. Council of Europe, Committee of Ministers: "Standard Minimum Rules for the Treatment of Prisoners", Resolution (73) 5, 1973.

10. Murray Cox: "Group psychotherapy in a secure setting", *Proc. Roy. Soc. Med.*, Vol. 69, March 1976, pp. 215-220.

11. Nick Davies: "Brain surgery used on Rampton patients", *The Guardian*, 17 October 1980.

12. David Dickson: "Psychosurgery supporters sued for malpractice", *Nature* Vol. 277, 18 January 1979, pp. 164-5.

13. *Faith and Science in an Unjust World*, Vol. 2, World Council of Churches, 1980, pp. 56-62.
14. Larry Gostin: "Ethical considerations of psychosurgery: the unhappy legacy of the pre-frontal lobotomy", with a commentary by Paul Bridges. *Journal of Medical Ethics*, Vol. 6, 1980, pp. 149-154. Also in the same issue an editorial "Surgery for the mind".
15. Gunn J., Robertson G., Dell S., & Way C.: *Psychiatric Aspects of Imprisonment*, (Chap. 1) Academic Press, London, 1978.
16. Seymour L. Halleck: "Legal and ethical aspects of behavior control", *The American Journal of Psychiatry*, 131: 4, April 1974, pp. 381-385.
17. Ed Harriman: "The brains behind the operation", (also 'The Rampton leucotomies"), *New Scientist*, 21 June 1979, pp.1002-3.
18. Ed Harriman: "Worries growing over anti-sex drug in prisons", *The Sunday Times*, 12 November 1978.
19. *Hazardous and irreversible treatments in psychiatry — who decides?*, report of a meeting of the Association of Psychiatrists in training held on 5 February 1980, Smith, Kline & French Laboratories Ltd., 1980.
20. L. Hollester: *Clinical Pharmacology of Psychotherapeutic Drugs*, Churchill Livingstone, New York, 1978. For general references on drugs in psychiatry.
21. Home Office, Department of Health: *Report of the Committee on Mentally Abnormal Offenders* (Chairman, Lord Butler), HMSO, 1975, Cmnd. 6244.
22. Home Office, Scottish Office, N. Ireland Office: *Report of the Committee of Inquiry into the United Kingdom Prison Services* (The May Report) London, HMSO, 1979, Cmnd. 7673.
23. Ian Kennedy: The Reith Lectures, "Unmasking medicine", "Great caution must be exercised in visiting the status of mentally ill on anyone", *The Listener*, 4 December 1980.
24. David Leigh: "How Ministry hardliners had their own way over prison units", *The Guardian*, 8 April 1980.
25. Robert J. Levine: "Clarifying the concepts of research ethics", *The Hastings Center Report*, June 1979, pp. 21-26.
26. Eliot Marshall: "Psychotherapy faces test of worth", *Science*, Vol. 207, 4 January 1980, pp. 35-36.
27 Mental Health Act 1959. HMSO.
28. Minutes of Evidence of the House of Commons Home Affairs Committee, 30 July 1980. HMSO, 1980.
29. "No bad faith by Home Secretary", The Times Law Report, Kynaston v. Secretary of State for Home Affairs and Another, *The Times*, 18 February 1981.
30. "Patient fails in claim for battery against doctor", The Times Law Report, Chatterton v. Gerson and Another, *The Times*, 6 February 1980.
31. David Patterson: "The violence of psychosurgery", *New Scientist*,

8 February 1979, pp. 374-376.
32. Melanie Phillips: "Hospital's use of drugs 'dangerous' ", *The Guardian*, 6 November 1979.
33. *Report of the Committee of Privy Councillors appointed to consider authorised procedures for the interrogation of persons suspected of terrorism*. Chairman Lord Parker. HMSO, 1972. Cmnd. 4901.
34. *Report of the Enquiry into allegations against the security forces of physical brutality in Northern Ireland arising out of events on 9th August, 1971*. Chairman: Sir Edmund Compton GCB, KBE. HMSO, 1971. Cmnd. 4823.
35. *Report to the Joint Working Party to formulate ethical guidelines for the conduct of programmes of behaviour modification* (Chairman: Prof. O. L. Zangwill), HMSO, 1980.
36. *Review of the Mental Health Act 1959*, HMSO, 1978, Cmnd. 7320.
37. Steven Rose: "All in the mind", *The Guardian*, 10 August 1978.
38. Dr. Barbara Sahakian: "Hyperactive children and the drug paradox", *New Scientist*, 2 November 1978, pp. 350-352.
39. Peter H. Schurr: "Psychosurgery", *British Journal of Hospital Medicine*, July 1973, pp. 53-60.
40. "Sex drugs avert gaol term", *The Guardian*, 25 April 1979.
41. Howard Sharron: "The scandal of St. Matthew's" *New Statesman*, Vol. 28, No. 2537, 2 November 1979, pp. 664-5.
42. Paul Sieghart: "Prisoners' Rights", *Law and Justice*.
43. *Statutory Registration of Psychotherapists*, Report of a Professions Joint Working Party, Tavistock Centre, 1978.
44. Martin Walker: "Broadmoor patient's fear of tranquillizers", *The Guardian*, 27 September 1980.
45. Michael White: "Minister denies drug abuse in prisons", *The Guardian*, 16 December 1978.
46. World Health Organisation: *Manual of the International Statistical Classification of Diseases, Injuries and Causes of Death*, Vol. 1, pp. 177-213, WHO, Geneva, 1977.

Appendix

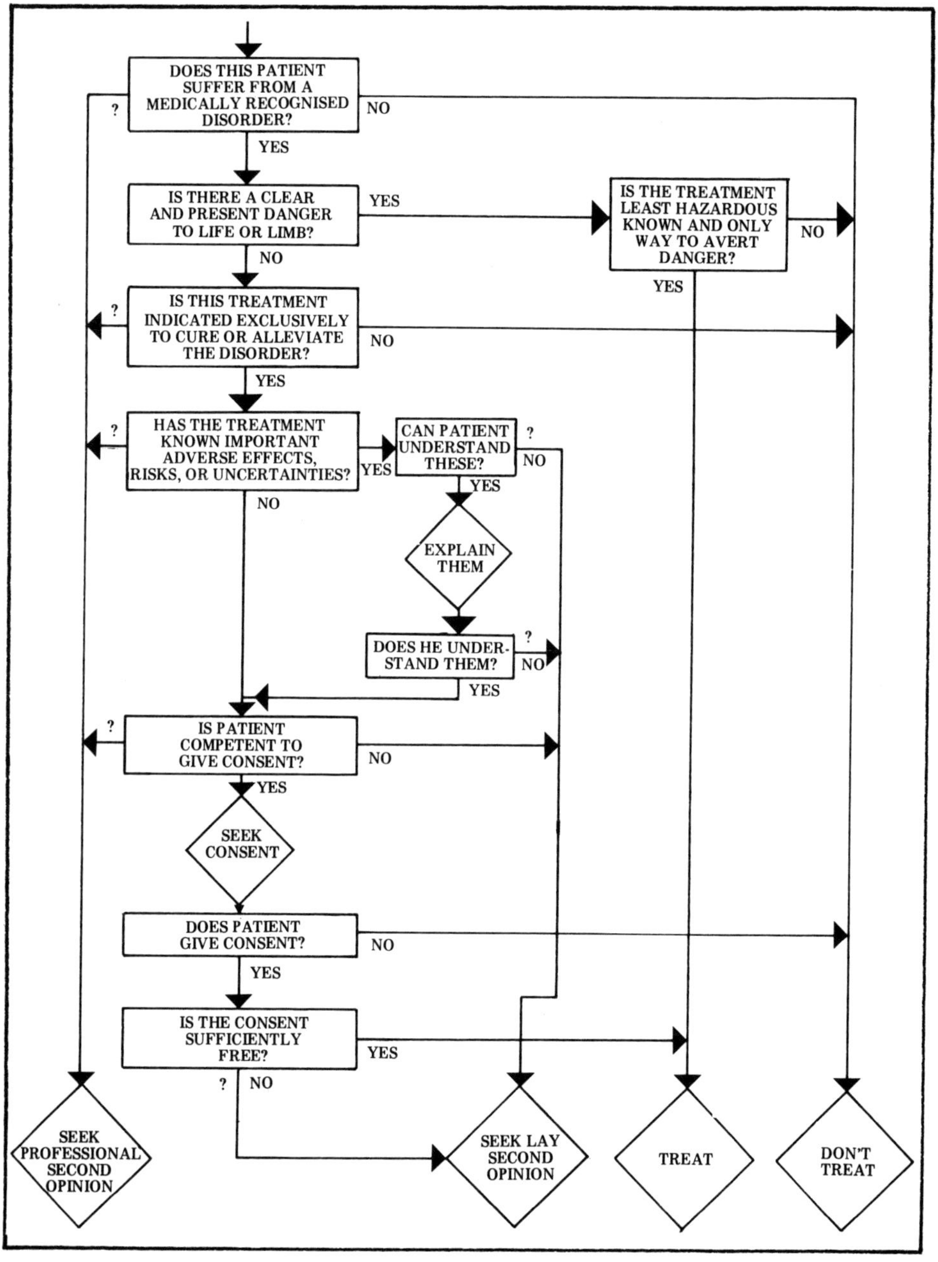

Appendix: Flow-chart for decisions involving consent